WALES

WALES

EDWARD THOMAS

Oxford New York

OXFORD UNIVERSITY PRESS

1983

Oxford University Press, Walton Street, Oxford OX2 6DP

London Glasgow New York Toronto
Delhi Bombay Calcutta Madras Karachi
Kuala Lumpur Singapore Hong Kong Tokyo
Nairobi Dar es Salaam Cape Town
Melbourne Auckland

and associates in
Beirut Berlin Ibadan Mexico City Nicosia

First published 1905
This edition first published 1924
First issued as an Oxford University Press paperback 1983

British Library Cataloguing in Publication Data

Thomas, Edward, 1878-1917
Wales.
1. Wales — Description and travel — 1801-1950
I. Title
914.29'0482   DA730
ISBN 0-19-281364-1

Printed in Great Britain by
Richard Clay (The Chaucer Press) Ltd
Bungay, Suffolk

CONTENTS

CHAPTER I

WALES

CHAPTER I

PRELIMINARY REMARKS ON MEN, AUTHORS, AND THINGS IN WALES

AMONG friends and acquaintances and authors, I have met many men who have seen and read more of Wales than I can ever do. But I am somewhat less fearful in writing about the country, inasmuch as few of them seem to know the things which I know, and fewer still in the same way. When I read their books or hear them speak, I am interested, pleased, amazed, but seldom am I quite sure that we mean the same thing by Wales; sometimes I am sure that we do not. One man writes of the country as the home of legends, whose irresponsibility puzzles him, whose naïveté shocks him. Another, and his name is legion, regards it as littered with dead men's bones, among which a few shepherds and miners pick their way without caring for the lover of bones. Another, of the same venerable and numerous family as the last, has admired the silver lake of Llanberis or blue Plynlimmon ; has been pestered by the pronunciation of Machynlleth, and has carried away a low opinion of the whole language because his own attempts at uttering it are unmelodious and even disgusting ; has fallen entirely in love with the fragrant Welsh ham, preferring it, in fact, to the curer and the cook. Others, who have not, as a rule, gone the length of visiting the persons they condemn, call the Welshmen thieving, lying, religious, and rebellious knaves. Others would repeat with fervour the verse which Evan sings in Ben Jonson's masque, *For the Honour of Wales*:

> And once but taste o' the Welsh mutton,
> Your English seep's not worth a button :

and so they would conclude, admitting that the trout are good when caught. Some think, and are not afraid of saying, that Wales will be quite a good place (in the season) when it has been chastened a little by English enterprise : and I should not be surprised were they to begin by introducing English sheep, though I hardly see what would be done with them, should they be cut up and exposed for sale. The great disadvantage of Wales seems to be that it is not England, and the only solution is for the malcontents to divide their bodies, and, leaving one part in their native land, to have the rest sent to Wales, as they used to send Welsh princes to enjoy the air of two, three, and even four English towns, at the same time and in an elevated position.

Then also there are the benevolent writers of books, who have for a century repeated, sometimes not unmusically, the words of a fellow who wrote in 1798, that the beauty of Llangollen "has been universally allowed by gentlemen of distinguished taste," and that, in short, many parts of Wales "have excited the applause of tourists and poets." Would that many of them had been provided with pens like those at the catalogue desks of the British Museum! Admirable pens! that may be put to so many uses and should be put into so many hands to-day and to-morrow. Admirable pens! and yet no one has praised them before. Admirable pens that will not write; and, by the way, how unlike those which wrote this:—

"Caldecot Castle, a grand and spacious edifice of high antiquity, occurs to arrest the observation of the passing stranger about two miles beyond the

new passage ; appearing at no great distance across
the meadows that lie to the left of the Newport
road.   The shattered remnants of this curious
example of early military architecture are still so far
considerable as to be much more interesting than
we could possibly have been at first aware, and
amply repaid the trouble of a visit we bestowed
upon it, in our return through Monmouthshire by
the way of Caldecot village.   In the distance truly
it does not fail to impress the mind with some idea
of its ancient splendour, for it assumes an aspect
of no common dignity : a friendly mantling of
luxuriant ivy improves, in an eminent degree, the
picturesque effect of its venerable mouldering
turrets ; and, upon the whole, the ruin altogether
would appear unquestionably to great advantage,
were it, fortunately for the admirers of artless
beauty, stationed in a more conspicuous situa-
tion, like the greater number of edifices of a
similar nature in other parts of the country."

The decency, the dignity, the gentlemanliness
(*circa* 1778), the fatuity of it, whether they tickle or
affront, are more fascinating than many better but
less portentous things.   There was, too, a Fellow
of the Royal Society who said in the last century
that, in the Middle Ages, St. Winifred's Well and

Chapel, and the river, and Basingwerk, must have been "worthy of a photograph."

Yet there are two others who might make any crowd respectable—the lively, the keen-eyed, the versatile Mr. A. G. Bradley, and George Borrow, whose very name has by this time absorbed and come to imply more epithets than I have room to give. From the former, a contemporary, it would be effrontery to quote. From the latter I allow myself the pleasure of quoting at least this, and with the more readiness because hereafter it cannot justly be said that this book does not contain a fine thing about Wales. Borrow had just been sitting (bareheaded) in the outdoor chair of Huw Morus, whose songs he had read "in the most distant part of Lloegr, when he was a brown-haired boy"; and on his way back to Llangollen, he had gone into a little inn, where the Tarw joins the Ceiriog brook. "'We have been to Pont-y-Meibion,' said Jones, 'to see the chair of Huw Morus,' adding, that the Gwr Boneddig was a great admirer of the songs of the Eos Ceiriog. He had no sooner said these words than the intoxicated militiaman started up, and, striking the table with his fist, said: 'I am a poor stone-cutter—this is a rainy day and I have come here to pass it in the best way I can. I am somewhat drunk, but though I am a poor stone-mason, a private in the militia, and not so sober as I should be, I can repeat more of the songs of the Eos than any man alive, however great a gentleman, however sober—more than Sir Watkin, more than Colonel Biddulph himself.'

"He then began to repeat what appeared to be poetry, for I could distinguish the rhymes occasion-ally, though owing to his broken utterance it was impossible for me to make out the sense of the words. Feeling a great desire to know what verses of Huw Morus the intoxicated youth would repeat, I took out my pocket-book and requested Jones, who was much better acquainted with Welsh pronunciation, under any circumstances, than my-self, to endeavour to write down from the mouth of the young fellow any verses uppermost in his mind. Jones took the pocket-book and pencil and went to the window, followed by the young man, scarcely able to support himself. Here a curious scene took place, the drinker hiccuping up verses, and Jones dotting them down, in the best manner he could, though he had evidently great difficulty to dis-tinguish what was said to him. At last methought the young man said, 'There they are, the verses of the Nightingale (Eos), on his deathbed. . . .'

". . . A scene in a public-house, yes! but in a Welsh public-house. Only think of a Suffolk toper repeating the deathbed verses of a poet; surely there is a considerable difference between the Celt and the Saxon?"

But the number is so great of sensible, educated men who have written on Wales, or would have written if business or pleasure or indolence or dislike of fame had not prevented them, that either I find it impossible to visit the famous places (and if I visit them, my predecessors fetter my capacity and actually put in abeyance the powers of the places), or, very rarely, I see that they were imperfect tellers of the truth, and yet feel myself unwilling to say an unpleasant new thing of village or mountain because it will not be believed, and a pleasant one because it puts so many excellent people in the wrong. Of Wales, therefore, as a place consisting of Llandudno, Llangammarch, Llanwrtyd, Builth, Barmouth, Penmaenmawr, Llanberis, Tenby, . . . and the adjacent streams and mountains, I cannot speak. At ——, indeed, I ate poached salmon and found it better than any preserver of rivers would admit; it was dressed and served by an Eluned (Lynette), with a complexion so like a rose that I missed the fragrance, and movements like those of a fountain when the south wind blows; and all the evening they sang, or when they did not sing, their delicate voices made "llech" and "llawr" lovely words: but I remember nothing else. At —— I heard some one playing *Là ci darem la mano*: and I remember nothing else. Then, too, there was ——, with its castle and cross and the memory of the anger of a king: and I remember that the rain outside my door was the only real thing in the world except the book in my hand; for the trees were as the dreams of one who does not care for dreams; the mountains were as things on a map; and the men and women passing were but as words unspoken and without melody. All I remember of —— is that, as I drew near to it on a glorious wet Sunday in winter, on the stony roads, the soles began to leave my boots. I knew no one there; I was to reach a place twelve miles ahead among the mountains; I was assured that nobody in the town would cobble on Sunday: and I began to doubt whether, after all, I had been wise in steadily preferring football boots to good-looking things at four times the price; when, finally, I had the honour of meeting a Baptist—a Christian—a man—who, for threepence, fixed my soles so firmly that he assured me they would last until I reached the fiery place to which he believed I was travelling, and serve me well there. I distrusted his theology, and have yet to try them on "burning marl," but they have taken me some hundreds of miles on earth since then.

It would be an impertinence to tell the reader what Llangollen is like, especially as he probably knows and I do not. Also, I confess that its very notoriety stupefies me, and I see it through a cloud of newspapers and books, and amid a din of applausive voices, above which towers a tremendous female form "like Teneriffe or Atlas unremoved," which I suppose to be Lady Eleanor Butler.

Nevertheless, I will please myself and the discerning reader by repeating the names of a few of the places to which I have never been, or of which I will not speak, namely, Llangollen, Aberglaslyn, Bettws-y-Coed, the Fairy Glen, Capel Curig, Colwyn, Tintern, Bethesda, Llanfairfechan, Llanrhaiadr, Llanynys, Tenby (a beautiful flower with a beetle in it), Mostyn, Glyder Fach and Glyder Fawr, Penmaenmawr, Pen-y-Gader, Pen-y-Gwryd, Prestatyn, Tremadoc, the Swallow Falls, the Devil's Bridge, the Mumbles, Harlech, Portmadoc, Towyn, and Aberdovey (with its song and still a poet there). I have read many lyrics worse than that inventory.

But there is another kind of human being—to use a comprehensive term—of which I stand in almost as much awe as of authors and those who know the famous things of Wales. I mean the lovers of the Celt. They do not, of course, confine their love—which in its extent and its tenuity reminds one of a very great personage indeed—to the Celt; but more perhaps than the Japanese or the Chinese or the Sandwich Islander the Celt has their hearts; and I know of one who not only learned to speak Welsh badly, but had the courage to rise at a public meeting and exhort the (Welsh-speaking) audience to learn their "grand mother tongue." Their aim and ideal is to go about the world in a state of self-satisfied dejection, interrupted, and perhaps sustained, by days when they consume strange mixed liquors to the tune of all the fine old Celtic songs which are fashionable. If you can discover a possible Celtic great-grandmother, you are at once among the chosen. I cannot avoid the opinion that to boast of the Celtic spirit is to confess you have it not. But, however that may be, and speaking as one who is

afraid of definitions, I should be inclined to call
these lovers of the Celt a class of "decadents," not
unrelated to Mallarmé, and of æsthetes, not unrelated to Postlethwaite.   They are sophisticated,
neurotic—the fine flower of sounding cities—often
producing exquisite verse and prose ; preferring
crême de menthe and *opal hush* to metheglin or
stout, and Kensington to Eryri and Connemara ;
and perplexed in the extreme by the Demetian
with his taste in wall-papers quite untrained.
Probably it all came from Macpherson's words,
"They went forth to battle and they always fell " ;
just as much of their writing is to be traced to
the vague, unobservant things in Ossian, or in the
proud, anonymous Irishman who wrote *Fingal* in
six cantos in 1813.   The latter is excellent in this
vein.   "Let none then despise," he writes, "the
endeavour, however humble, now made, even by
the aid of fiction, to throw light upon the former
manners and customs of *one of the oldest and
noblest nations of the earth.*   That *once we were,* is
all we have left to boast of ; that *once we were,*
we have record upon record. . . . We yet can
show the stately pharos where waved the chieftain's
banner, and the wide ruin where the palace stood—
the palace once the pride of ages and the theme

of song—once *Emuin a luin Aras Ullah.*" The
reader feels that it is a baseness to exist. Mr.
John Davidson, who, of course, is as far removed
from the professional Celt as a battle-axe from a
toothpick, has put something like the fashionable
view majestically into the mouth of his " Prime
Minister " :

> . . . That offscouring of the Eastern world,
> The melancholy Celt, whom Latin, Greek,
> And Teuton drove through Europe to the rocks,
> The utmost isles and precincts of the sea ;
> Who fight for fighting's sake, and understand
> No meaning in defeat, having no cause
> At heart, no depth of purpose, no profound
> Desire, no inspiration, no belief ;—
> A twilight people living in a dream,
> A withered dream they never had themselves,
> A faded heirloom that their fathers dreamt :
> How much more happy these had they destroyed
> The spell of life at once, and so escaped
> An unregarded martyrdom, the consciousness
> Of inefficience and the world's contempt.

But it is probably true that when one has said
that the typical Celt is seldom an Imperialist, a
great landowner, a brewer, a cabinet minister, or
(in Wales, at least) a member of the Salvation
Army, one has exhausted the list of his weak-
nesses ; and that not greatly wanting to be one of
these things, he has endeared himself to those to-day

who have set their hearts on gold and applause
and have not gained them, and those few others
who never sought them. I heard of a pathetic,
plausible stockbroker's clerk the other day, who,
having spent his wife's money and been at last
discovered by his tailor, took comfort in studying
his pedigree, which included a possibly Welsh Lewis
high upon the extreme right. He was sufficiently
advanced in philology to find traces of an Ap' in
his name, which was Piper, and he could repeat
some of Ossian by heart with great emotion and
less effect. I prefer the kind of Celt whom I met
in Wales one August night. It was a roaring wet
night, and I stepped into the shelter of a bridge to
light a pipe. As I paused to see if it was dawn yet,
I heard a noise which I supposed to be the breathing
of a cow. My fishing-rod struck the bridge ; the
noise ceased, and I heard something move in the
darkness close by. I confess that my pipe went
out when, without warning, a joyous, fighting
baritone voice rose and shook the bridge with the
words :

> Through all the changing scenes of life,
>   In trouble and in joy,
> The praises of my God shall still
>   My heart and tongue employ.

The voice sang all the verses of the hymn, and

then laughed loudly, yet with a wonderful serenity.
Then a man stood up heavily with a sound like a
flock of starlings suddenly taking flight. I lit a
match and held it to his face and looked at him,
and saw a fair-skinned, high-cheek-boned face,
wizened like a walnut, with much black hair
about it, that yet did not conceal the flat, straight,
eloquent mouth. He lit a match and held it to my
face, and looked at me and laughed again. Finding that I could pronounce Bwlch-y-Rhiw, he was
willing to talk and to share the beer in my satchel.
And he told me that he had played many parts—
he was always playing—before he took to the road:
he had been a booking-office clerk, a soldier, a
policeman, a gamekeeper, and put down what
he called his variability to "the feminine gender."
He would not confess where he had been to school,
and his one touch of melancholy came when, to
show that he had once known Latin, he began to
repeat, in vaguely divided hexameters, the passage in
the *Aeneid* which begins *Est in conspectu Tenedos.*
For he could not go on after *At Capys* and was
angry with himself. But he recalled being caned
for the same inability, and laughed once more.
Every other incident remembered only fed his
cheerfulness. Everything human had his praise,—

General Buller in particular. I cannot say the
same of his attitude towards the divine. His con-
versation raised my spirits, and I suppose that the
bleared and dripping dawn can have peered on few
less melancholy men than we. " Life," said he, " is
a plaguey thing : only I don't often remember it."
And as he left me, he remarked, apologetically, that
he "always had been a cheerful ——, and couldn't
be miserable," and did me the honour of supposing
that in this he resembled me.

He went off singing, in Welsh, something not
in the least like a hymn to a fine victorious hymn
tune, but had changed, before I was out of hearing,
to the plaintive, adoring " Ar hyd y nos." And I
remembered the proverbial saying of the Welsh,
that "the three strong ones of the world" are "a
lord, a headstrong man, and a pauper."

Having heard and read the aforesaid authors,
tourists, higher philatelists, and lovers of the Celt,
I need hardly say, firstly, that I have come under
their influence ; secondly, that I have tried to avoid
it ; and thirdly, that I am not equal to the task of
apportioning the blame between them and myself
for what I write.

And, first, let me ease my memory and pamper

my eyes, and possibly make a reader's brain rever-
berate with the sound of them, by giving the names
of some of the streams and lakes and villages I have
known in Wales. And among the rivers, there are
Ebbw and Usk, that cut across my childhood with
silver bars, and cloud it with their apple flowers
and their mountain-ash trees, and make it musical
with the curlew's despair and the sound of the
blackbird singing in Eden still; and Towy and
Teivy and Cothi and Ystwyth; and, shyer streams,
the old, deserted, perhaps deserted, pathways of the
early gods, the Dulais and Marlais and Gwili and
Aman and Cenen and Gwenlais and Gwendraeth
Fawr and Sawdde and Sawdde Fechan and Twrch
and Garw; and those nameless but not unremem-
bered ones (and yet surely no river in Wales but has
a name if one could only know it well enough) that
crossed the road like welcomed lingerers from some
happier day, flashing and snake-like, and ever about
to vanish and never vanishing, and vocal all in reed
or pebble or sedge, some deep enough for a sewin,
others too shallow to wash the dust from the little
pea-like toes of the barefooted child that learns
from them how Nile and Ganges flow, and why
Abana and Pharpar were dear, and why these are
more sweet; and there is Llwchwr, whose voice is

bright in constant shadow ; and Wye ; and the little river in a stony valley of Gower which at first reminded me, and always reminds me, of the adventure of Sir Marhaus, Sir Gawaine, and Sir Uwaine.

" And so they rode, and came into a deep valley full of stones, and thereby they saw a fair stream of water ; above thereby was the head of the stream a fair fountain, and three damosels sitting thereby. And then they rode to them, and either saluted other, and the eldest had a garland of gold about her head, and she was threescore winter of age or more, and her hair was white under the garland. The second damosel was of thirty winter of age, with a circlet of gold about her head. The third damosel was but fifteen year of age, and a garland of flowers about her head. When the knights had so beheld them, they asked them the cause why they sat at that fountain ? ' We be here, ' said the damosels, ' for this cause : if we may see any errant knights, to teach them unto strange adventures ; and ye be three knights that seeken adventures, and we be three damosels, and therefore each one of you must choose one of us ; and when ye have done so we will lead you unto three highways, and there each of you shall choose a way and his damosel with him. And this day twelve-month ye must meet here again, and God send you your lives, and thereto ye must plight your troth.' 'This is well said,' said Sir Marhaus." And no other than a Welsh story-teller could have made that clear picture of the three damosels.

And there is Severn in its wild and unnoted childhood, its lovely and gallant youth, its noble and romantic prime, as it leaves Wales and passes Shrewsbury, the pattern of all famous streams—

Fluminaque antiquos subterlabentia muros;

and its solemn, grey, and mighty and worldly-wise old age, listening to its latest daughter the Wye, where it has

A cry from the sea, a cry from the mountain;

and Clwyd and Conway and Ceiriog and Aled and Dovey, streams that remember princes and bards; and the little waters flowing from Cwellyn Lake, of which a story is told.

Near the river which falls from Cwellyn Lake, they say that the fairies used to dance in a meadow on fair moonlit nights. One evening the heir to the farm of Ystrad, to which the meadow belonged, hid himself in a thicket near the meadow. And while the fairies were dancing, he ran out and carried off one of the fairy women. The others at once disappeared. She resisted and cried, but he led her to his home, where he was tender to her, so that she was willing to remain as his maid-servant. But she would not tell him her name. Some time afterward he again saw the fairies in the meadow and overheard one of them saying, "The last time we met here, our sister Penelope was snatched away from us by one of the mortals." So he returned and offered to marry her, because she was hard-working and beautiful. For a long time she would not consent; but at last she gave way, on the condition "that if ever he should strike her with iron, she would leave him and never return to him again." They were happy together for many years; and she bore him a son and a daughter; and so wise and active was she, that he became one of the richest men of that country, and besides the farm of Ystrad, he farmed all the lands on the north side of Nant-y-Bettws to the top of Snowdon, and all Cwm Brwynog in Llanberis, or about five thousand acres. But one day Penelope went with him into a field to catch a horse; and as the horse ran away from him, he was angry and threw the bridle at him, but struck Penelope instead. She disappeared. He never saw her again, but one night afterward he heard her voice at his window,

asking him to take care of the children, in these
words :

Oh, lest my son should suffer cold,
Him in his father's coat enfold :
Lest cold should seize my darling fair,
For her, her mother's robe prepare.

These children and their descendants were called
the Pellings, says the teller of the tale ; and "there
are," he adds, "still living several opulent and
respectable persons who are known to have sprung
from the *Pellings*. The best blood in my own veins
is this fairy's."

And of lakes, I have known Llyn-y-Fan Fach,
the lonely, deep, gentle lake on the Caermarthen
Fan, two thousand feet high, where, if the dawn
would but last a few moments longer, or could one
swim but just once more across, or sink but a little
lower in its loving icy depths, one would have such
dreams that the legend of the shepherd and the
lady whom he loved and gained and lost upon the
edge of it would fade away : and Llyn Llech Owen,
and have wondered that only one legend should be
remembered of those that have been born of all the
gloom and the golden lilies and the plover that
glories in its loneliness ; for I stand in need of a
legend when I come down to it through rolling
heathery land, through bogs, among blanched and

lichened crags, and the deep sea of heather, with a few
flowers and many withered ones, of red and purple
whin, of gorse and gorse-flower, and (amongst the
gorse) a grey curling dead grass, which all together
make the desolate colour of a "black mountain";
and when I see the water for ever waved except
among the weeds in the centre, and see the water-
lily leaves lifted and resembling a flock of wild-fowl,
I cannot always be content to see it so remote, so
entirely inhuman, and like a thing a poet might
make to show a fool what solitude was, and as it
remains with its one poor legend of a man who
watered his horse at a well, and forgot to cover it
with the stone, and riding away, saw the water
swelling over the land from the well, and galloped
back to stop it, and saw the lake thus created and
bounded by the track of his horse's hooves; and thus
it is a thing from the beginning of the world that
has never exchanged a word with men, and now
never will, since we have forgotten the language,
though on some days the lake seems not to have
forgotten it.   And I have known the sombre
Cenfig water among the sands, where I found the
wild goose feather with which I write.

And I have seen other waters; but least of
them all can I forget the little unnecessary pool

that waited alongside a quiet road and near a grim, black village. Reed and rush and moss guarded one side of it, near the road; a few hazels over-hung the other side; and in their discontented writhing roots there was always an empty moor-hen's nest, and sometimes I heard the bird hoot unseen (a sound by which the pool complained, as clearly as the uprooted trees over the grave of Polydorus complained), and sometimes in the un-kind grey haze of winter dawns, I saw her swim-ming as if vainly she would disentangle herself from the two golden chains of ripples behind her. In the summer, the surface was a lawn of duckweed on which the gloom from the hazels found something to please itself with, in a slow meditative way, by showing how green could grow from a pure emerald, at the edge of the shadow, into a brooding vapourish hue in the last recesses of the hazels. The smell of it made one shudder at it, as at poison. An artist would hardly dare to sit near enough to mark all the greens, like a family of snaky essences, from the ancient and mysterious one within to the happy one in the sun. When the duckweed had dissolved in December, the pool did but whisper that of all things in that season, when

Blue is the mist and hollow the corn parsnep,

it alone rejoiced. It was in sight of the smoke
and the toy-like chimney-stacks of the village, of
new houses all around, and of the mountains. It
had no possible use—nothing would drink of it.
It did not serve as a sink, like the blithe stream
below. It produced neither a legend nor a brook.
It was a whole half-acre given up to a moorhen
and innumerable frogs. It was not even beautiful.
And yet, there was the divinity of the place,
embodied, though there was no need for that, in
the few broken brown reeds that stood all the
winter, each like a capital Greek *lambda*, out of
the water. When the pool harboured the image
of the moon for an hour in a winter night, it
seemed to be comforted. But when the image
had gone, the loss of that lovely captive was
more eloquent than the little romantic hour.
And I think that, after all, the pool means the
beauty of a pure negation, the sweetness of
utter and resolved despair, the greatness of Death
itself.

And I have been to Abertillery, Pontypool,
Caerleon, infernal Landore, Gower, Pontardulais,
Dafen, Llanedi, Llanon (where only the little Gwili
runs, but good children are told that they shall go
to Llanon docks), Pen-y-Groes, Capel Hendre, Maes-

y-bont, Nantgaredig, Bolgoed, Pentre Bach, Bettws, Amanford, Llandebie, Pentre Gwenlais, Derwydd, Ffairfach, Llandeilo, Tal-y-Llychau, Brynamman, Gwynfe, Llanddeusant, Myddfai, Cil-y-Cwm, Rhandir Mwyn, and the farms beyond,—Maes Llwyn Fyddau, Bwlch-y-Rhiw, Garthynty, Nant-yr-ast, Blaen Cothi, Blaen Twrch,—Llanddewi Brefi, Tregaron, Pont Llanio, Llanelltyd, Bettws Garmon, Bala, Aber Dusoch. . . . And I have crossed many " black " mountains, and Gareg Lwyd, Gareg Las, the Banau Sir Gaer, Crugian Ladies, Caeo, Bryn Ceilogiau, Craig Twrch, and Craig-y-Ddinas. . . .

The chapels and churches, Siloh, Ebenezer, Llanedi, Llandefan, Abergwesyn, Llanddeusant, . . . but I dare not name them lest I should disturb some one's dreams, or invite some one to disturb my own. They are all in the admirable guide-books, which say nothing of the calm and the nettles and the shining lizards and the sleepy luxurious Welsh reading of the lessons at —— ; and the wet headstones at ——, where you may lean on any Sunday in the rain and hear the hymn take heaven by storm, and quarrel melodiously upon the heights, and cease and leave the soul wandering in the rain as far from heaven as

Paolo and Francesca in their drifts of flame; and
——, white and swept and garnished, and always
empty, and always lighted by a twilight four
hundred years old, the door being open and ready
to receive some god or goddess that delays; and
Soar at ——, so blank, lacking in beauty and even
in ugliness,—so blank that when one enters, the
striving spirit will not be content, and perforce
takes flight and finds an adventure not unlike that
of the man who was once returning from Beddgelert
fair by a gloomy road, and saw a great and splendid
house conspicuously full of gaiety in a place where
no such house had seemed to stand before; and
supposing that he had lost his way, he asked and
was given a lodging, and found the chambers
bright and sounding with young men and women
and children, and slept deeply in a fine room, on a
soft white bed, and on waking and studying his
neighbourhood, saw but a bare swamp and a tuft
of rushes beneath his head.

And there is Siloh at ——, standing bravely,—
at night, it often seems perilously,—at the end of
a road, beyond which rise immense mountains
and impassable, and, in my memory, always the
night and a little, high, lonely moon, haunted for
ever by a pale grey circle, looking like a frail

creature which one of the peaks had made to sail for his pleasure across the terrible deeps of the sky. But Siloh stands firm, and ventures once a week to send up a thin music that avails nothing against the wind ; although close to it, threatening it, laughing at it, able to overwhelm it, should the laugh become cruel, is a company of elder trees, which, seen at twilight, are sentinels embossed upon the sky—sentinels of the invisible, patient, unconquerable powers : or (if one is lighter-hearted) they seem the empty homes of what the mines and chapels think they have routed ; and at midnight they are not empty, and they love the mountain rain, and at times they summon it and talk with it, while the preacher thunders and the windows of the chapel gleam.

And there is ——, where an ancient, unwrinkled child used to talk in gentle, melancholy accents about hell to an assembly of ancient men who sometimes muttered " Felly, felly," as men who had heard it so often that they longed to be there and to taste and to see ; where the young men and maidens sang so lustily and well that I wondered the minister never heard them, or, hearing, understood them. To the children, when they listened, his mild ferocity did but put an edge on the bird'snesting of the day before and the day after. When they did not listen, some of them looked through the windows and saw heaven as fresh and gaudy, in the flowers of a steep garden close by, as in the coloured pictures of apostles and lambs on their bedroom walls; but chiefly in the company of delicate lime trees that stood above the garden, on a grassy breast of land. The fair, untrodden turf below them shone even when the sun was not with it. The foliage of all the limes, in autumn, ripened together to the same hue of gold. It burned and was cool. It flamed and yet had something in it of the dusk. It was the same as when, many years ago, two children saw in it some fellowship with the coloured windows at Llandaff, and with the air of an old library that had "golden silence and golden speech" over the door. And the trees seemed to be a council of blessed creatures devising exquisite enjoyments and plotting to outwit the preacher. They might be not ill-chosen deputies of leisure, health, and contemplation, and all that fair and reverend family. In the cool gloom at the centre of the foliage sat also Mystery, with palms linked before her eyelids, unlinking them but seldom, lest seeing might shut out visions.

CHAPTER II

THE best way into Wales is the way you choose, provided that you care. Some may like the sudden modern way of going to sleep at London in a train and remaining asleep on a mountain-side, which has the advantage of being the most expensive and the least surprising way. Some may like to go softly into the land along the Severn, on foot, and going through sheath after sheath of the country, to reach at last the heart of it at peaty Tregaron, or the soul of it on Plynlimmon itself. Or you may go by train at night; and at dawn, on foot, follow a little stream at its own pace and live its fortnight's life from mountain to sea.

Or you may cross the Severn and then the lower Wye, and taking Tredegar and Caerleon alternately, or Rhigws and Landore, or Cardiff and Lantwit, or the Rhondda Valley and the Vale of Neath, and thus sharpening the spirit, as an epicure may sharpen his palate, by opposites, find true Wales everywhere, whether the rivers be ochre and purple with corruption, or still as silver as the fountain dew on the mountain's beard; whether the complexions of the people be pure as those of the young cockle-women of Penclawdd, or as heavily superscribed as those of tin-platers preparing to wash. Or you may get no harm by treading in the footsteps of that warm-blooded antiquarian, Pennant, who wrote at the beginning of his tours in Wales: "With obdurate valour we sustained our independency . . . against the power of a kingdom more than twelve times larger than Wales: and at length had the glory of falling, when a divided country, beneath the arms of the most wise and most warlike of the English monarchs." That "we" may have saved the soul even of an antiquarian.

But the entry I best remember and most love was made by a child whom I used to know better than I have known anyone else. He disappeared, after a slow process of evanishment, several years ago: and I will use what I know as if it were my own, since the first person singular will help me to write as if I should never be subjected to the dignity of print,—as if I were addressing, not the general reader, but some one who cared.

At a very early age, I (that is to say, he, *bien entendu*) often sat in a room in outer London, where I now see that it was probably good to be. It was always October there, and the yellow poplar leaves were always falling. And so also there was always a fire—a casket in which emeralds and sapphires contended with darker spirits continually. Where are the poplars now? Where the leaves which loved the frost that spoiled them at last? Where the emeralds and sapphires—and the child? There were late October twilights that seemed so mighty in their gentleness and so terrible in their silence that they alarmed the child with fear of desolation, until the spell was suspended by lighted lamps and drawn curtains and fearless voices of elder persons, though one could draw the curtains and see the thing still, and oneself, and the very fire, outside in its embrace. And still

> The jealous ear of night eave-dropped our talk.

I think those twilights have overwhelmed all at last, and they have their way with child and trees and fire. But they have spared one thing, which even in those days was more puissant than the fire, though they have left their marks upon it, and now it seems a less mighty thing if one goes to it soberly, too critically, or even too cheerfully. For a picture hung in the room, and the last October sunlight used to fall upon it when the silence set in. The picture meant Wales.

In the foreground, a stream shone with ripples in the midst, and glowed with foam among the roots of alders at the edge. Branches with white berries overhung the stream; and there were hornbeams and writhen oaks; and beyond them, a sky with a shaggy and ancient storm in it, and wrestling with that, and rising into it, the ruins of an Early English chancel. The strength and anger and tenderness and majesty of it were one great thought. I still think that could deeds spring panoplied from thoughts, and could great thoughts of themselves do anything but flush the cheek, such a simply curving landscape as this would be at the bidding of one of those great thoughts that empty all the brain. . . . Under one of the columns by the chancel, the artist meant to have drawn vaguely a pile of masonry and a muscular ivy stem. And that was the point of the picture, because it seemed to be a kneeling knight, with one forearm on an oval shield and the other buried in his beard, and his head bent. I suppose that the thought that it was a knight, and that the knight was Launcelot, first came as I looked at the picture once, straight from a book where I had been reading:

"Then Sir Launcelot departed, and when he came to the Chapel Perilous, he alighted, and tied his horse to a little gate. And as soon as he was within the churchyard he saw on the front of the Chapel many fair, rich shields turned upside down; and many of the shields Sir Launcelot had seen knights have before; with that he saw standing by him thirty great knights, more by a yard than any man that he had ever seen, and all these grinned and gnashed at Sir Launcelot; and when he saw their countenances he dreaded them sore, and so put his shield afore him, and took his sword in his hand ready to do battle; and they were all armed in black harness, ready with their shields and swords drawn. And when Sir Launcelot would have gone through them they scattered on every side of him, and gave him the way to pass; and therewith he waxed all bold, and entered into the Chapel, and there he saw no light but a dim lamp burning, and then he was aware of a corse covered with a cloth of silk. And as Sir Launcelot stooped

down and cut a piece of the cloth away, the earth
quaked, and he was afraid. . . ."

And the picture was a picture of the Chapel
Perilous; and thus out of a poor story-book and
a dear picture and the dim poplars in the dim
street, I made a Launcelot who was not merely an
incredible mediæval knight of flesh and armour,
but a strange immortal figure that lived and was
desirable and friendly in the grey rain of a suburb
in the nineteenth century.

This was the beginning of the creation of Wales.
Or shall I say that it was the beginning of the
discovery? Let the reader decide, with the help
of the explanation, that I use the words as I
should use them of a play of Shakespeare's, or a
picture of Titian's, or any other living thing which
grows and changes and is born again, in age after
age, as certainly and as elusively as the substance
of a waterfall is changed; even in one moment
these things are never the same to any two
observers, backward or advanced, egotistical or
servile, blind or keen. . . .

Looking back, the artistry of time makes
it appear that soon after I had become certain
that the painter had somehow caught Launcelot

kneeling at the foot of the column, I reached Wales.

There I saw one of the Round Tables of Arthur, but also a porpoise hunt in the river close by; and the porpoise threshed the water so that the shining spray now hides the Round Table from my view. And I heard the national anthem of Wales: and at first I cowered beneath the resolved and terrible despair of it, forgetting that—

> In every dirge there sleeps a battle-march;

so that I seemed to look out from the folds of a fantastic purple curtain of heavily embroidered fabric upon a fair landscape and an awful sky; and I know not whether the landscape or the sky was the more fascinating in its mournfulness.

> And I heard sounds of insult, shame, and wrong,
> And trumpets blown for wars,—

and it was of Arthur's last battle that I dreamed. But the sky cleared, and I seemed to let go of the folds of the curtain and to see a red dragon triumphing and the shielded Sir Launcelot again; and next, it was only a tournament that I saw, and there were careless ladies on high among the golden dust. And, at last, I could once more think happily of the little white house where I

lived, and the largest and reddest apples in all the
world that grew upon the wizened orchard, and
the smoked salmon and the hams that perfumed
the long kitchen, and all the shining candlesticks,
and the wavy, crisp, thin leaves of oaten bread
that were eaten there with buttermilk: and the
great fire shook his rustling sheaf of flames and
laughed at the wind and rain that stung the
window-panes; and sometimes a sense of triumph
arose from the glory of the fire and the vanity of
the wind, and sometimes a sense of fear lest the
fire should be conspiring with the storm. That
also was Wales—a meandering village street, the
house with the orchard, and a white river in sight
of it, and the great music of the national anthem
hovering over it and giving the whole a strange
solemnity.

Just beyond the village, but not under the same
solemn sky, I see an island of apple trees in spring,
which in fact belongs to a somewhat later year.
It was reached by a mile of winding lane that
passed the slender outmost branches of the village,
and lastly, a shining cottage, with streaked and
mossy thatch, and two little six-paned windows,
half-filled with many-coloured sweets, and boasting
one pane of bottle-glass. Outside sat an old woman;

her moist, grey, hempen curls framing a cruel
face which had been made by three or four swift
strokes of a hatchet; her magnificent brown eyes
seeming to ponder heavenly things and really
looking for half-pence. A picture would have
made her—wringing her hands slowly as if she
were perpetually washing, or sitting bolt upright
and pleased with her white apron — a type of
resigned and reverend and beautiful old age. On
the opposite side of the road was a white and
thatched piggery, half the size of the house; and
alongside of it, a neat, moulded pile of coal-dust,
clay, and lime, mixed, for her ever-burning fire.
The pigs grunted; the old woman, who would
herself watch the slaughtering, sat and was pleased,
and said, " Good morning," and " Good afternoon,"
and " Good evening " as the day went by, except
when the children were due to pass to and from
school, with half-pence to spend.

Just beyond this dragon and its house, an important road crossed the lane, which then narrowed
and allowed the hedgerow hazels to arch over it and
let in only the wannest light to the steep, stony
hedge-bank of whin and grass and fern and violets.
Little streams ran this way and that, under and over
and alongside the lane, and at length a larger one

was honoured by a bridge, the parapet covered
with flat, dense, even turf. The bridge made way
for a wide view, and to invite the eye a magpie
flew away from the grassy parapet with wavy
flight to a mountain side.

Between the bridge and the mountain, and in
fact surrounded by streams which were heard
although unseen, was an island of apple trees.

There were murmurs of bees. There was a
gush and fall and gurgle of streams, which could
be traced by their bowing irises. There was a
poignant glow and fragrance of flowers in an air
so moist and cold and still that at dawn the earliest
bee left a thin line of scent upon it. Beyond, the
mountain, grim, without trees, lofty and dark,
was clearly upholding the low blue sky full of slow
clouds of the colour of the mountain lambs or of
melting snow. This mountain and this sky, for
that first hour, shut out, and not only shut out but
destroyed, and not only destroyed but made as if
it had never been, the world of the old woman, the
coal-pits, the schools, and the grown-up persons.
And the magic of Wales, or of Spring, or of
childhood made the island of apple trees more
than an orchard in flower. For as some women
seem at first to be but rich eyes in a mist of

complexion and sweet voice, so the orchard was
but an invisible soul playing with scent and colour
as symbols. Nor did this wonder vanish when
I walked among the trees and looked up at the
blossoms in the sky. For in that island of apple
trees there was not one tree but was curved and
jagged and twisted and splintered by great age, by
the west wind, or by the weight of fruit in many
autumns. In colour they were stony. They were
scarred with knots like mouths. Some of their
branches were bent sharply like lightning flashes.
Some rose up like bony, sunburnt, imprecating
arms of furious prophets. One stiff, gaunt bole
that was half hid in flower might have been Ares'
sword in the hands of the Cupids. Others were
like ribs of submerged ships, or the horns of an
ox emerging from a skeleton deep in the sand of
a lonely coast. And the blossom of them all
was the same, so that they seemed to be Winter
with the frail Spring in his arms. Nor was I
surprised when the first cuckoo sang therein, since
the blossom made it for its need. And when a
curlew called from the mountain hopelessly, I
laughed at it.

When I came again and saw the apple trees in
flower, the island was very far away, and the

unseen cuckoo sang behind a veil and not so suitably as the curlew. There was something of the dawn in the light over it, though it was mid-day; and I could hardly understand, and was inclined to melancholy, until chance brought into my head the poem of the old princely warrior poet Llywarch Hên, and out of his melancholy and mine was born a mild and lasting joy. He sang:

Sitting high upon a hill, to battle is inclined
My mind, but it does not impel me onward.
Short is my journey, my tenement is laid waste.

Sharp is the gale, it is bare punishment to live.
When the trees array themselves in gay colours
Of Summer, extremely ill am I this day.

I am no hunter, I keep no animal of the chase,
I cannot move about:
As long as it pleases the cuckoo, let her sing.

The loud-voiced cuckoo sings with the dawn,
Her melodious notes in the dales of Cuawg:
Better than the miser is the lavish man.

At Aber Cuawg the cuckoos sing,
On the blossom-covered branches;
Woe to the sick that hears their contented notes.

At Aber Cuawg the cuckoos sing.
The recollection is in my mind,
There are that hear them that will not hear them again.

Have I not listened to the cuckoo on the ivied tree?
Did not my shield hang down?
What I loved is but vexation; what I loved is no more.

And I thought that perhaps it is even true, as Taliesin sang, that "A man is wont to be oldest when born, and younger all the time," and that the apple flowers did but remind me of old capacities laid waste.

These little things are the opening cadences of a great music which I have heard, and which is Wales. But I have forgotten the whole, and have echoes of it only, when I hear an old Welsh song, when I am trying to catch a trout, or am eating bread and butter and white cheese, and drinking pale tea, in a mountain farm. . . . One echo of it I had strangely in Oxford, when, entertaining an old wise gipsy, and asking him of his travels, and whether he had been in Wales, he meditated for a long time, and then sang in an emotionless and moving tone the "Hen wlad fy nhadau," up there among the books, the towers, and the stars. I have had a vision of a rose. But my memory possesses only the doubtful and withered dustiness of a petal or two.

CHAPTER III

A FARMHOUSE UNDER A MOUNTAIN, A FIRE,
AND SOME FIRESIDERS

HAVING passed the ruined abbey and the orchard, I came to a long, low farmhouse kitchen, smelling of bacon and herbs and burning sycamore and ash. A gun, a blunderbuss, a pair of silver spurs, and a golden spray of last year's corn hung over the high mantelpiece and its many brass candlesticks; and beneath was an open fireplace and a perpetual red fire, and two teapots warming, for they had tea for breakfast, tea for dinner, tea for tea, tea for supper, and tea between. The floor was of sanded slate flags, and on them a long many-legged table, an oak settle, a table piano, and some Chippendale chairs. There were also two tall clocks; and they were the most human clocks I ever met, for they ticked with effort and uneasiness: they seemed to think and sorrow over time, as if they caused it, and did

41

not go on thoughtlessly or impudently like most
clocks, which are insufferable; they found the
hours troublesome and did not twitter mechanically
over them; and at midnight the twelve strokes
always nearly ruined them, so great was the effort.
On the wall were a large portrait of Spurgeon,
several sets of verses printed and framed in memory
of dead members of the family, an allegorical tree
watered by the devil, and photographs of a bard
and of Mr. Lloyd George. There were about
fifty well-used books near the fire, and two or three
men smoking, and one man reading some serious
book aloud, by the only lamp; and a white girl was
carrying out the week's baking, of large loaves, flat
fruit tarts of blackberry, apple, and whinberry, plain
golden cakes, large soft currant biscuits, and curled
oat cakes. And outside, the noises of a west wind
and a flooded stream, the whimper of an otter, and
the long, slow laugh of an owl; and always silent,
but never forgotten, the restless, towering outline
of a mountain.

The fire was—is—of wood, dry oak-twigs
of last spring, stout ash sticks cut this morning, and brawny oak butts grubbed from the
copse years after the tree was felled. And I
remember how we built it up one autumn, when

the heat and business of the day had almost let
it die.

We had been out all day, cutting and binding
the late corn. At one moment we admired the
wheat straightening in the sun after drooping in
rain, with grey heads all bent one way over the
luminous amber stalks, and at last leaning and
quivering like runners about to start or like a wind
made visible. At another moment we admired the
gracious groups of sheaves in pyramids made by
our own hands, as we sat and drank our buttermilk
or ale, and ate bread and cheese or chwippod (the
harvesters' stiff pudding of raisins, rice, bread, and
fresh milk) among the furze mixed with bramble and
fern at the edge of the field. Behind us was a place
given over to blue scabious flowers, haunted much
by blue butterflies of the same hue ; to cross-leaved
heath and its clusters of close, pensile ovals, of a
perfect white that blushed towards the sun ; to a
dainty embroidery of tormentil shining with un-
varied gold ; and to tall, purple loosestrife, with
bees at it, dispensing a thin perfume of the kind
that all fair living things, plants or children,
breathe.

What a thing it is to reap the wheat with your
own hands, to thresh it with the oaken flail in the

misty barn, to ride with it to the mill and take your
last trout while it is ground, and then to eat it with
no decoration of butter, straight from the oven!
There is nothing better, unless it be to eat your
trout with the virgin appetite which you have won
in catching it. But in the field, we should have
been pleased with the plainest meal a hungry man
can have, which is, I suppose, barley bread and a
pale "double Caermarthen" cheese, which you cut
with a hatchet after casting it on the floor and
making it bounce, to be sure that it is a double
Caermarthen. And yet I do not know. For even
a Welsh hymnist of the eighteenth century, in trans-
lating "the increase of the fields," wrote avidly of
"wheaten bread," so serious was his distaste for
barley bread. But it was to a meal of wheaten
bread and oat cake, and cheese and onions and
cucumber, that we came in, while the trembling
splendours of the first stars shone, as if they also
were dewy like the furze. Nothing is to be compared with the pleasure of seeing the stars thus in
the east, when most eyes are watching the west,
except perhaps to read a fresh modern poet, straight
from the press, before any one has praised it, and to
know that it is good.

As we sat, some were singing the song

"Morwynion Sir Gaerfyrddin." Some were looking out at the old hay waggon before the gate.

Fine grass was already growing in corners of the wrecked hay waggon. Two months before, it travelled many times a day between the rick and the fields. Swallow was in the shafts while it carried all the village children to the field, as it had done some sixty years ago, when the village wheelwright helped God to make it. The waggoner lifted them out in clusters ; the haymakers loaded silently ; the waggon moved along the roads between the swathes ; and, followed by children who expected another ride, and drawn by Swallow and Darling, it reached the rick that began to rise, like an early church, beside the elms. But hardly had it set out for another load than Swallow shied ; an axle splintered and tore and broke in two, near the hub of one wheel, which subsided so that a corner of the waggon fell askew into the tussocks, and the suspended horse-shoe dropped from its place. There the mare left it, and switched her black tail from side to side of her lucent, nut-brown haunches, as she went.

All day the waggon was now the children's own. They climbed and slid and made believe that they were sailors, on its thin, polished timbers. The grass had grown up to it, under its protection. Before it fell, the massive wheels and delicate curved sides had been so fair and strong that no one thought of its end. Now, the exposed decay raised a smile at its so recent death. No one gave it a thought, except, perhaps, as now, when the September evening began, and one saw it on this side of the serious, dark elms, when the flooded ruts were gleaming, and a cold light fell over it from a tempestuous sky, and the motionless air was full of the shining of moist quinces and yellow fallen apples in long herbage; and, far off, the cowman let a gate shut noisily; the late swallows and early bats mingled in flight; and, under an oak, a tramp was kindling his fire. . . .

Suddenly in came the dog, one of those thievish, lean, swift demi-wolves, that appear so fearful of meeting a stranger, but when he has passed, turn and follow him. He shook himself, stepped into the hearth and out and in again. With him was one whose red face and shining eyes and crisped hair were the decoration with which the wind invests his true lovers. A north wind had risen and given the word, and he repeated it: let us have a fire.

So one brought hay and twigs, another branches

and knotted logs, and another the bellows. We made an edifice worthy of fire and kneeled with the dog to watch light changing into heat, as the spirals of sparks arose. The pyre was not more beautiful which turned to roses round the innocent maiden for whom it was lit; nor that more wonderful round which, night after night in the west, the clouds are solemnly ranged, waiting for the command that will tell them whither they are bound in the dark blue night. We became as the logs, that now and then settled down (as if they wished to be comfortable) and sent out, as we did words, some bristling sparks of satisfaction. And hardly did we envy then the man who lit the first fire and saw his own stupendous shadow in cave or wood and called it a god. As we kneeled, and our sight grew pleasantly dim, were we looking at fireborn recollections of our own childhood, wondering that such a childhood and youth as ours could ever have been; or at a golden age that never was? . . . The light spelt the titles of the books for a moment, and the bard read Spenser aloud, as if forsooth a man can read poetry in company round such a fire. So we pelted him with tales and songs. . . .

And one of the songs was "The Maid of Landybie," by the bard, Watcyn Wyn. Here

follows the air, and a translation which was made
by an English poet. The naïveté of the original has
troubled him, and the Welsh stanza form has driven
him to the use of rhymeless feminine endings; but
I think that his version will, with the air, render
not too faintly the song I heard.

THE MAID OF LANDYBIE

Air: Y Ferch o Blwyf Penderyn.

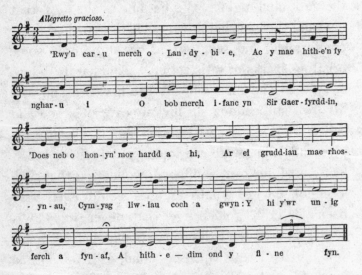

I love a maid of Landybie
And it is she who loves me too.
Of all the women of Caermarthen
None is so fair as she, I know.
White and red are her cheeks' young roses,

The tints all blended mistily ;
She is the only maid I long for,
And she will have no lad but me.

I love one maid of Landybie
And she too loves but one, but one ;
The tender girl remains my faithful,
Pure of heart, a bird in tone.
Her beauty and her comely bearing
Have won my love and life and care,
For there is none in all the kingdoms
Like her, so blushing, kind, and fair.

While there is lime in Craig-y-Ddinas ;
While there is water in Pant-y-Llyn ;
And while the waves of shining Loughor
Walk between these hills and sing ;
While there's a belfry in the village
Whose bells delight the country nigh,
The dearest maid of Landybie
Shall have her name held sweet and high.

When we are by this fire, we can do what we
like with Time, making a strange solitude within
these four walls, as if they were cut off in time as
in space from the great world by something more
powerful than the night ; so that, whether Llewelyn
the Great, or Llewelyn the Last, or Arthur, or
Kilhwch, or Owen Glyndwr, or the most recent
prophet be the subject of our talk, nothing in-
trudes that can prevent us for the time from being
utterly at one with them.   They sing or jest or

make puns; they talk of hero and poet as if they had met them on the hills; and as the poet has said, "Folly would it be to say that Arthur has a grave."

In such a room are legends made, if made at all. In fact, I lately saw a pretty proof of it.

The valley in which the farmhouse lies is not so fortified that some foreign things of one kind and another cannot enter. And a miner or a youth on holiday from London brought a song of Bill Bailey to the ears of one of the children of the house, a happy, melancholy boy named Merfyn. The elders caught it for a day or two, and though the song does not recommend itself to those who are heirs to "Sospan bach" and "Ar hyd y nos," the name of the hero stuck. The child asked who he was, and could get no answer. When anything happened about the farm that could not easily be explained, it was jestingly said that Bill Bailey was at the bottom of it. The child seriously caught up the name and the mystery, and applied it with amusing and strange effect. Thus, when he had asked who made the mushrooms in the dawn, and was not satisfied, he himself decided, and with pride and joy announced, that they were Bill Bailey's work. Looking into the fire one night, and seeing

faces that he could not recognise among the
throbbing heat, he saw Bill Bailey, as he surmised.
Thus is a new solar hero being bred.   The last
news is that he made Cader Idris and Orion and
the Pleiades, and that the owls cry so sadly because
he is afoot in the woods.

And yet, if we are so unwise as to draw back
the curtain from the window at night, the illusion
of timelessness is broken for that evening, and in
the flower-faced owl by the pane, in the great hill
scarred with precipices, and ribbed with white and
crying streams, with here and there a black tree
disturbed and a very far-off light, I can see nothing
but the past as a magnificent presence besieging
the house.   At such times the legends that I
remember most are those of the buried and unfor-
gotten lands.   What I see becomes but a symbol
of what is now invisible.   And sometimes I dream
of something hidden out there and elaborating
some omnipotent alcahest for the world's delight
or the world's bane ; sometimes, as when I passed
Llanddeusant and Myddfai, I could see nothing
that was there, because I was thinking of what
had been long ago.   There is still a tradition on
the coast that Cardigan Bay now covers a country
that was once populous and fair and rich.   The

son of a prince of South Wales is said to have had charge of the floodgates on the protecting embankment, and one night the floodgates were left open at high tide, while he slept with wine, and the sea was over the corn. "Seithenyn the Drunkard let in the sea over Cantre-'r-Gwaelod, so that all the houses and lands contained in it were lost. And before that time there were in it sixteen fortified towns superior to all the towns and cities in Wales, except Caerlleon on the Usk. And Cantre-'r-Gwaelod was the dominion of Gwyddno, King of Cardigan, and this event happened in the time of Ambrosius. And the people who escaped from that inundation came and landed in Ardudwy, the country of Arvon, the Snowdon mountains, and other places not before inhabited." . . . The sands in some places uncover the roots of an old forest. According to one tradition the flood took place during a feast. The harper suddenly foresaw what was to happen and warned the guests; but he alone escaped. There is also a tradition that Bala Lake covers old palaces. It is said that they have been seen on clear moonlit nights, when the air is one sapphire, and that a voice is heard saying, "Vengeance will come"; and another voice, "When will it come?"

and again the first voice saying, " In the third generation." For a prince once had a palace where the lake is. He was cruel and persisted in his cruelty, despite a voice that sometimes cried to him, "Vengeance will come." One night there was a bright festival in the palace, and there were many ladies and many lords among the guests, for an heir had just been born to the prince. The wine shone and was continually renewed. The dancers were merry and never tired. And a voice cried, "Vengeance." But only the harper heard ; and he saw a bird beckoning him out of the palace. He followed, and if he stopped, the bird called, "Vengeance." So they travelled a long way, and at last he stopped and rested, and the bird was silent. Then the harper upbraided himself, and turned, and would have gone back to the palace. But he lost his way, for it was night. And in the morning he saw one calm large lake where the palace had been ; and on the lake floated the harper's harp. . . .

This fire, in my memory, gathers round it many books which I have read and many men that I have spoken with among the mountains—gathers them from coal-pits and tin-works and schools and

chapels and farmhouses and hideous cottages,
beside rivers, among woods; and I have drawn a
thin line round their shadows and have called the
forms that came of it men, and their "characters"
follow.

CHAPTER IV

TWO MINISTERS, A BARD, A SCHOOLMASTER, AN INNKEEPER, AND OTHERS

Mr. Jones, the Minister

JONES is a little, thin, long-skulled, black-haired, pale Congregational minister, with a stammer and a squint. He has a book-shelf containing nothing but sermons and theology, which he has read, and the novels of Sir Walter Scott, which he hopes to read. I suppose he believes in metempsychosis. He is accustomed to say that everything is theology—which is fine; and that theology is everything—which is hard. He tries to love man as well as God, and succeeds in convincing every one of his honesty, generosity, and industry. In the care of souls he fears no disease or squalor or shape of death. But there is a condescension about his ways with men. He calls them the worldliest of God's creatures. But with the Divine he is happy

and at ease, and in his pulpit seems to sit on the
right hand. Then his Biblical criticism is absent
as if it had never been, and he sees the holy things
at once as clearly as Quarles and as mystically as
Herbert or Crashaw. He speaks of them with the
enthusiasm of a collector or of a man of science
dealing with a bone or a gas. Like them, he sees
nothing but the subjects of the moment. He
loves them as passionately and yet with a sense of
possession. He gives to them the adoration which
he seems wilfully to have withheld from women,
pageantry, gardens, palaces—which his speech
would have adorned. He lavishes upon them his
whole ingenious heart, so that, to those used to
the false rhetoric and dull compliment of ordinary
worshippers, there is in his sermons something
fantastical, far-fetched, or smelling of the lamp.
If he has to describe something naked or severe,
he must needs give them a kind of voluptuousness
by painting the things which they lack, and the
lack of which makes them what they are. With
Herbert, he might repeat :

> My God, where is that ancient heat towards thee,
> Wherewith whole shoals of Martyrs once did burn,
>   Besides their other flames ? doth Poetry
> Wear Venus' livery ? only serve her turn ?
> Why are not Sonnets made of thee ? and lays

Upon thine altar burnt? Cannot thy love
Heighten a spirit to sound out thy praise
As well as she? Cannot thy Dove
Outstrip their Cupid easily in flight?
  Or, since thy ways are deep, and still the same,
  Will not a verse run smooth that bears thy name?
Why doth the fire which by thy power and might
  Each breast does feel, no braver fuel choose
  Than that, which one day worms may chance refuse?
Sure, Lord, there is enough in thee to dry
  Oceans of ink; for as the Deluge did
  Cover the Earth, so does thy Majesty;
Each cloud distils thy praise, and doth forbid
Poets to turn it to another use.
  Roses and lilies speak thee: and to make
  A pair of cheeks of them, is thy abuse.
Why should I women's eyes for crystal take?
Such poor invention burns in their low mind
  Whose fire is wild, and does not upward go
  To praise, and on thee, Lord, some note bestow.
Open the bones, and you shall nothing find
  In the best face but filth; when, Lord, in thee
  Thy beauty lies in the discovery.

It is no matter to him that to the uninspired audience his holy persons appear only exquisite marionettes. His sermons are all of his love for them. Could one leave out the names of prophet and evangelist, they might seem to be addressed to earthly beauties. No eyebrow ever awakened more glowing praise. He takes religion, as he does his severe morality, like a sensuous delight. One might think from his epithets that he was an æsthete, except that he is so abandoned.

When he ventures to speak of men, their very virtues and vices are all handled in such a way that they seem to be his own imaginations. Thus, his drunkard is as unreal and as terrible as a chimera. The words are those of a man who has conceived a drunkard in his own brain, and then, seeing the real thing, has preferred his own conception, and shunned the poor human imitation. Still, he speaks of religious things, of incidents in the life of David or Christ or the Maries, as if he had seen, for example, the Holy Family in some misty barn among his own hills. I have even heard him introduce a farmer whittling a flail of hazel sticks and binding it with willow thongs, in a picture of that scene. This quaintness and clearness are perhaps the result of his not quite healthy asceticism. But even by the farmhouse fire he makes use of them, and will speak of the red or brown hair of scriptural characters, and even of the grey hair and shining eyes of Charity. In hunger or weariness or pain, common people sometimes see things thus: he never sees them otherwise. In the chapel they delight the older labourers, and yet fail because they vanish in the cold night air and "leave not a rack behind." Some hearers, on the other hand, sicken at them, when the blood is noisy in the breast and the brain is warm, as they sicken at drugs.

It is not, therefore, surprising that at one time he had gorgeous earthly dreams. But with an oddity of which nothing will cure him, he is much troubled by this pomp which he desires not to see save in celestial things. And now he allows sleep nightly but a brief victory over him.

The Landlord of the "Cross Inn"

A very pretty companion for Jones was Owen, the innkeeper, a robust man of words, who called himself the preacher's best customer, because he needed so much of his charity.

He was a perfect Celt, according to the English superstition. For never was there such a failure who was also such a swaggerer as he. He had fair hair, blue eyes, and a small, elegant beard, which

> Business could not make dull, nor passion wild.

He was bullied by a contemptuous wife; he was ridiculed by all his regular customers, rallied by the rest. But the beard was always neat and fair, a symbol of his unconquerable mind. No matter how he was trodden down, he smelt sweet. He had

humour, for he could laugh at himself, though he
lacked the common gift of being able to laugh at
others, and had no repartee. The more lusty the
Saturday night thrusts at him, the more vivid was
his reply, and it was commonly a piece of egoism
and self-exposure, which, if not so long and so
wonderfully draped, would have called for a repeti-
tion of the very blow he was parrying. Once when
he had been sold up and had little more than a wife
and a walking-stick in the world, and his position
attracted some trifling compliments and condolences
from his old harriers, he stood up, and, wielding his
stick and motioning to his wife to be silent, gave
an inventory of the things he had lost with such
decoration as would have abashed an auctioneer.
There is a Welsh proverb, " A Welshman keeps
nothing until he has lost it"; and the now invisible
and inaccessible furniture called up such a tumult
of admiration that he cared not that it was no
longer his. How rich he looked ! As the words
flowed on and it was time for his hearers to be
going, it was clear that if he had forgotten anything, he had invented more; but though he ended
in no better company than that of his wife, who
picked something from his coat and held it between
the tips of two fingers for his humiliation, he but

wiped his forehead and cursed because he had forgotten the ancient horse-trappings of brass that used to hang over the mantelpiece at the —— Arms.

His voice, whether he sang or spoke, was of wide range and exquisite adjustment, and he spoke with care and gusto, as if he loved his native tongue. Under its influence, he respected nobody of any importance. Thus, he was once pretty justly thrashed; when, having tired his chastiser by his patience, he remarked at great length that he supposed the other did not know who he was, and the splendour of his manner overcame his heated companion. No sooner had he got home than he gave a rapturous description of how one had given another a thrashing down the road. He did it so well that he was asked whether he was the beater. "No," said he bravely, "it happened that I was beat."

Had he lost by a bargain, had he taken a bad coin unawares, had he been worsted in argument, he could so rant that he moved every one, and himself obviously first of all, and made the worse appear the better. He kept a genealogical tree in constant use by pruning and watering, and though there was not only a prince but a poet in it, I think he gloried less in the old splendour of his family than in the length of its fall, as who should say he had once been so high that he was "from morn to dewy eve" in falling.

When first I saw him, he had just come into the "Cross Inn." It was mid-day ; the weather was cold and wet ; and since he never liked to see a man drinking by himself, and the shepherds coming down from the mountains to market had called pretty often, he was not sober. He told me that his was a fine house—the finest in the village, and therefore in the county ; and that it had not paid the former tenant well, who had, in fact, sold but eighteen gallons of beer in a month. He was going to do better than that, he said ; to make a beginning, he was going to drink that quantity himself. I asked for brandy. He had not a drop, and explained that he had a weakness for it himself—took a drop very often ; and that therefore, to get out of temptation, he had finished his stock on the night before. "But," said he, "I have upstairs such a bed as you—pardon me—never slept in yet."

"I have no doubt," said I, and sat down.

But when he heard that I was walking across Wales, and had therefore tried many beds, he insisted that I should see the thing. It was the finest in the village—in the county—in Wales—"I don't see why I should not say in the whole world." Truly it was a noble bed, in a great, empty, raftered, uncarpeted room; the wood all darkened oak, with a dusky gleam; the hangings ample and of a rich crimson stuff; the purity of the linen splendid. If a royal person or a poet had not slept in it, "that was their misfortune." He stood by, awed and reverent, beholding the bed. I was not his equal in eloquence, and he echoed my praise with an elaborate "of course": and for the sake of hearing some of the words he loved, he finally invited me to spend a night in the bed, "as his guest," so he magnificently said.

All his family were of the same temper. His father and mother had gone to London years ago, and, at seventy years of age, to the infirmary of a workhouse. . . .

The aged paupers sat in a long, grey, motionless, and silent row—like a sculptured frieze, or like persons expecting to be photographed—under the wall of a church. Before them was a strip of grass, one emerald half of which shone so that it seemed of an element like flame; for it was pure, insubstantial colour; and into this, as the paupers saw, the tide of the shadow of the church gradually ate. Beyond the grass was the infirmary, and alongside it a yellow road, and on that a hearse. Watching this and the paupers, a crowd of persons, with uninterested, inquisitive eyes and bowler hats, stuck their noses through the railings which ran between the busy street and the infirmary. Motor cars brayed, hooves clattered.

Presently three men carried out a coffin, containing the remains of Mrs. Owen, and shoved it into the hearse. "God love me, what a coffin!" said one of the crowd. But the frieze of paupers were silent and motionless in the long grey row— all but the husband of the corpse. He, like the others, seemed to stare at the hearse with fixed gaze, and in a loud voice he remembered what a bonny woman the corpse had been, and in particular how, while a travelling musician played in the village street, when she was past fifty years of age, she had locked herself into the kitchen and danced, having spread a mat to deaden the clicking of her merry clogs; and he had watched her, unobserved. The story and his uncontrolled, bleating voice raised a laugh under the bowler hats; and the old men lifted their heads and straightened themselves and laughed; and most loudly and grimly of all laughed Owen, while he remembered the cottage in sight of the beacons of Breconshire; and the hearse rolled out and the crowd removed.

Mr. Rowlands, the Minister

Rowlands, another minister, is six feet and two inches in height, seventeen stone in weight, and has a voice which is in proportion. When he stands up, one supposes that he can never sit down; when he sits down, one supposes that he can never stand up. Every one of his attitudes seems to be final. Only when he is moving is his ponderosity a little less than divine; for he moves with an odd briskness, so that, from behind, he is like a large schoolboy on some urgent business. His mind is subject to similar changes of aspect. In domestic life no one is less awful than he; and were he not goodtempered, cheerful, frolicsome, and humorous as well, he would be one of the most mirth-provoking of mankind. On children he leaves no impression but that of weight, and in spite of his black clothes, he once reminded a child (with a shrill voice) of Atlas upholding the world.

In his everyday life he is a learned, happy child. His curiosity is matched by his credulity. He is the victim not only of tradesmen, but of beggars.

He cannot keep his coat clean, and that he sews on his own buttons is apparent from the fact that he seldom has more than one or two of those decorations. He knows every one in his neighbourhood— miners, farmers, parsons, and the resident Englishmen—and knows and loves them so well that he never condemned any one except for cruelty. For he seems to have started life with such a strong belief in the sinfulness of men, that he has ever since been pleased and surprised by this one's goodness and the amiability of that one's badness. He might, in truth, have spoken of himself in something like the words of that fine, possibly Welsh poet of the seventeenth century, Thomas Traherne:

A learned and a happy ignorance
        Divided me
    From all the vanity,
From all the sloth, care, pain, and sorrow that advance
    The madness and the misery
Of men.   No error, no distraction I
Saw soil the earth or overcloud the sky.

I knew not that there was a serpent's sting
        Whose poison shed,
    On men, did overspread
The world; nor did I dream of such a thing
    As sin, in which mankind lay dead.
They were all brisk and living wights to me,
Yea, pure and full of immortality.

> Joy, pleasure, beauty, kindness, glory, love,
>   Sleep, day, life, light,
>   Peace, melody, my sight,
> My ears and heart did fill and freely move.
>   All that I saw did me delight.
> The universe was then a world of treasure,
> To me an universal world of pleasure. . . .

His own verses, by the way, are not so good, for, like all Welsh ministers, he writes a hundred lines of verse every day, perhaps to avoid being thought singular.

He makes a fine figure of Charity in his old age, with his preoccupied blue eyes under a brow that is marked only by three lines like three beams thrown upward by a sun. He has a large, joyous, curving mouth, side-whiskers, careless beard, large feet.

He has but one touch of sentiment. Nearly half a century ago he fell in love with a pretty woman, and unsuccessfully; yet, though she is known to be married and still alive, he has come to have for her memory a grandfatherly tenderness, regarding her as a white and careless girl, in spite of time. For the rest, so warm and radiant is he, that I remember the peculiarity of Kai. "When it rained hardest, whatever he carried remained dry for a handbreadth above and a handbreadth below his hand , and when his companions were coldest, it was to them as fuel with which to light their fire."

But in the pulpit—whether it is a whim or an atonement or merely a recollection of his years at a theological college—he always makes an attempt to dust the wrinkles of his waistcoat. In every other way he makes his week-day self incredible to a stranger. He justifies and makes use of his size more than any man I ever saw. Seeing him in the pulpit, it seems fitting that he should live there day and night, so necessary a pillar is he to the dull, small chapel, though, when holding out his arms, as often he does, he threatens to demolish the little arches and poor windows and to create something more splendid in their place. Going there once in his absence, a visitor remarked to a deacon that they had made some changes in the building ; and asking what had gone from there, he was told, "Oh, only Mr. Rowlands."

Standing there, he undertakes to speak on behalf of the Deity, whose ways he explains, and by a magnificent self-conceit supposes that his own stature and voice are fitting symbols to mortals incapable of apprehending things more august. For a time, indeed, during the singing of the

hymns, there is a geniality as of lightning about his
face. He smiles; he tosses his head with the joy
of the song, and may even be supposed to feel, not
without sympathy, that the mighty music says
things which were not dreamed of by prophets or
apostles.

When he reads a lesson, it is plain to see that
above all other Gods he loves "the Lord that
smiteth." He opens his mouth and rejoices in the
rich and massy Welsh. He makes no attempt at
mere clear reading, which would be of no use to an
imaginative audience, that is familiar with the
Bible; but, raising and lowering his voice, now
hurrying as if to a precipice where all will be over-
thrown, now creeping as if he feared what is to
come, he makes the chapter anew, creating it as if
he were sculptor or musician. I suppose he uses
nearly as many musical notes as if he sang; but
the result differs from singing, as prose from poetry;
and so noble is the prose that it suggests only one
possible answer to the question which, like a school-
man, he once asked, Whether the music of the
spheres be verse or prose? Yet, if the note of the
lesson is melancholy, full of the dreariness of moving over the void and creating, the note of the
sermon is triumphant, or if not triumphant it is

minatory, or if not minatory it is scornful, and at times a listener expects to see him wrapped in a cloud and carried away from an undeserving and purblind race.

The medium of what English people would call his rhetoric is the "hwyl," an exuberant, impassioned, musical modulation of the voice, and, to compare great things with small, comparable to the very finest intoning to which has been added (if we can suppose it) a lyrical, egotistical indulgence in all moods of pity, scorn, tenderness, anger, sorrow, joy, anxiety and hope. It can be familiar or lofty. It is as powerful as harp and song together; and the force of it often arises from the fact that what is heard is rather the musical accompaniment of the man's thought than the thought itself. Hence its terrible and lovely purposes, and the many sentiments with which it is shot, and the dubiousness of the loftier passages, as in the verses which the bards recited before Arthur and only one man understood them, except that they were in Arthur's praise.

I have seen him so thunder that I thought of the Llewelyns and Glyndwr, and forgot that the castles fester no longer with Englishmen, and

aerea ramis
dependet galea et prato gravia arma quiescunt,

and for the moment, thought he was a man. No
actor ever stormed and swelled so, because no actor
yet played the part which he played. It was a
chant; yet it was too uncontrollable for a chant.
If you call it declamation, you must admit that to
declaim a man shall first go to Medea, that she

> Having drawn that weakness from his limbs
> Which torpid now and chilly there abode,
> Through every vacant artery may force
> The green and joyous sap of thriving plants,—
> Juice of crushed stalks mixed with their ropy gums,
> And purpled bright with strength from berry and grape,
> Full of a stinging, swift, and masterful
> Vivacity.

For the blood of a declaimer of seventy does not
travel so by ordinary ways. Nor can a declaimer,
as he does, build up for the imagination an earth,
with sky and mountains, within a little chapel, for
the sake of showing how the lightning vaults and
impales the unjust man. At other times his words
rise up and circle and make fantastic architecture,
as real as dreams, for the terror of the soul that for
the time is forced to dwell therein. And though
the substance of his sermon is but anecdote, biblical
reference, exhortation, warning, picturesque logic
built upon some simple religious theme, men and
women weep under this divine bullying. A man,

listening outside the chapel, put his hand to his head to make sure that his hat was on, so stiffly his hair stood up.

"Then the earth shook and trembled; the foundations also of the hills moved and were shaken, because he was wroth. . . .

"He bowed the heavens also, and came down: and darkness was under his feet.

"And he rode upon a cherub, and did fly: yea, he did fly upon the wings of the wind.

"He made darkness his secret place; his pavilion round about him were dark waters and thick clouds of the skies. . . ."

Once he paused long, towards the end of a sermon, while the thunder withdrew with a terrible solemnity which he envied; and he did not hesitate to follow the thunder with the words, "It has been said," and so to end.

The Poacher

One who used to come in late, years ago, was Gwilym Pritchard, the poacher.

I wish to make a nice distinction between poachers and poachers. The man who is nothing but a poacher I regard as one only in the strict literal sense. Such a man is rare to-day. Formerly

he went to the woods as another man went to the
Bar. He lived like a gentleman upon other men's
venison, and was beneath the pleasure of salt-pork
broth. He would swagger about the hamlet with
a deer on his back. The deer was but a carcass
at sixpence the pound to him. He has lately
stooped to dictate his autobiography, which may
be bought over the counter. A less majestical
note was never sounded. He turned gamekeeper,
and no doubt touched his cap for half-a-sovereign,
and stared at his palm for a crown. He is, in
short, "one of God's creatures." But the nobler
one I have in mind seemed to bear high office in
the scheme of the natural world. A mighty man,
capable of killing anything and of sparing anything
too, he was a true scholar in his kind. The pedants
who peep and botanise and cry "allium" or
"cnicus" to one another in the awful woods, and
the sublime enthusiasts who cannot see the earth
for the flowers, were equally beneath him. He
would give twelve hours a day at least to the open
air, as a scholar to his books. Thus he had
acquired a large erudition which would probably
have exhausted a whole field of inquiry if written
down. It is fortunate that faultless observers
like this hand down nothing to posterity, since it

leaves us in these latter days free to feel ourselves
discoverers when we come upon what hundreds
have known during the last thousand years. In
the case of this man, the knowledge came out not
so much in speech—of which he was economical—
as in infinite tact,

> Wearing all that weight
> Of learning lightly like a flower.

It was shown in the way he stepped in
the woods, in the way he laid his ear to the
bare ground (not the grass) to ascertain a distant noise of footsteps. I have seen him lose a
wood-pigeon by an interrupted aim, and, standing
without sound or motion, shoot the bird, that
returned to its branch, enchanted by the absence
of hostile sounds; for his very clothes were more
the work of nature than the tailor, and matched
the trees like a hawk or a November moth. His
belief in the earth as a living thing was almost
a superstition. I shall not forget how he took
me to a hilltop one autumn day, when the quiet
gave birth to sound after sound as we listened
and let our silence grow. By a process of elimina-
tion he set aside the wind, the birds, the falling
leaves, the water, and tried to capture for my
sake the low hum which was the earth making

music to itself. And what I heard I can no more describe than the magic of an excellent voice when once it is silent. "Depend upon it, that means something," he said. "And now——" there was a sharp report and a hare that I had not noticed bounded as if it had fallen from a great height, and lay dead.

Having been caught once, I remarked that his captor must have been a clever man. "A fool," he replied—"a fool. He'd been after me a hundred times, and I had fooled him all but once." It was at one time his practice to deliver a tithe of his poached game at the cottages of the sick, infirm, or poor, *as a present from the Squire*, a notoriously ungenerous man. His occupation had made him indifferent to the future or the past. None ever chattered less about past happiness and future pain. He seemed to owe a duty to the present moment of which he partook as if he were eating ripe fruit. Even a piece of drudgery or a keen sorrow never drove his intelligence backward or forward; pain he took as some take medicine, on trust. Thus he was a small, though not a poor, talker. Venturing once to greet him pleasantly with the long beginning of a story, when I found him seated without any visible occupation, and noticing his irritation, I said that I had supposed he was not doing anything; to which he answered "Yes, nothing!" and continued. At one time of his life he heard that a considerable sum of money had been left to him. A year later, the foundering of a ship left his fortunes unchanged; and on the afternoon of the news, he shot every pigeon at which he raised his gun. Birds of prey he would never shoot, even to show his skill. Jackdaws were always spared; he used to say that there was "a bit of God" in that bird. It was noticeable, too, that here and there he spared game birds, though he despised the race. I have seen him raise his gun and drop it again, not without a sigh as the bird flew off, observing that there was "something in the bird" which stayed his hand. In men, as in birds and beasts, he was anxious to see individuality, and loved the creature that possessed and used it. The only time I ever saw him use contempt was towards a beggar who had soiled his calling by theft. A good beggar, a good thief, anything beyond which "the force of nature could no further go," he reverenced. And he was a good poacher, glorying in the name. He died polishing the white steel on his gun.

Llewelyn, the Bard

Of Llewelyn, the bard, I cannot decide whether he most loves man or men. He is for ever building castles in the air and filling them with splendid creatures, whom he calls men. Then he laments that he cannot find any like them on hill or in valley : when, straightway, he will meet some human being, old friend or passing stranger, on the road or in a shop, and away go the phantoms of his castles, and he is wild in adoration of the new thing he has found. His grandmother, by the way, was called a fairy's child, though the truth seems to have been that her mother was a gipsy girl. Perhaps that is why he has no creed but many creeds, and was looked upon with great favour by the Calvinists until they found that he liked the Church as well. Yet I think that he likes men truly because they remind him of something he has read or dreamed, or because they make him dream ; herein somewhat resembling the fellow who paid much court to another because he reminded him of the late Duke of ——, and he was a lover of dukes. Or he is like some that have seen processions of phantoms and say that sometimes the phantoms are simply fairies speaking

an unknown tongue, but that sometimes several
have the faces and voices of some among the dead
whom they used to know. Why he is so glad to
be among us at the farmhouse I have not discovered, but I suppose we remind him of Hebrew
prophets or Greekish kings, for of our established
merits he takes no thought.

I think he wastes so much pity for Annie of
Lochroyan that other maids find him passionless,
and he grows tender over Burd Ellen and Cynisca
as their lovers never did. Arthur and Gwalchmai
and Gwenhwyvar, the most unreal and unliving of
all the persons of literature, please him most. In
a world where all things are passing, he loves best
those things which, having past and having left a
ghost of fame behind, can live for ever in minds
like his. In London he saw but a place where
marsh and river and woods had been and might be
again ; or where

> Sometimes a lily petal floated down
> From dear, remote pools to the dreary town ;

where the gulls flew over in the mournful January
light ; where a few friends had fires and lamps and
books—their light faintly flickering in tremendous
gloom and making one faint reality in the place ;
where wind and rain sometimes brought the past

again; for the very touch of rain and wind beckoned
to him, as it is fabled that the foam driven from
waters that cover old towns will draw the unwary
whom it touches into the deeps.

He himself professes to care only for his own
childhood and youth; only he is aware, as not
every one is, that the childhood began in Eden,
and is ages old, so that, after all, the few years that
make middle age do not count for much. His life
and his way of looking at it remind me of a story
of a young Eastern prince. Every day, from his
early childhood, a story-teller had told him a tale.
But, soon after he was sixteen, the story-teller
came to him, and, falling on his knees, told him
that he had no more stories to tell. The young
prince fell into a rage and swore that he would kill
the man if, in a week, he had no new story ready.
And the story-teller, who was very old and unwilling to die, went into the desert and neither ate
nor drank, and made a plan by which to save his
life. So he returned to the young prince, who
asked if he had a new story, and he said that he
had. And the prince bade him tell the story; and
he began to speak, and told the prince the story
which he had told him first, when he was a small
child; and the prince was pleased. And until the

old man died, he never told a story which he had
not told before; and the prince was always pleased.

His poetry, if it could be understood, might be
counted great, and perhaps it is so in a world where
trees and animals are reverenced in a way which is
hardly dawning here. He is a kind of mad Blake.
He sees the world from among the stars, and those
who see it from an elevation of five or six feet, and
think that they see it as it really is, are not satisfied.
He would make human the stars and seasons; he
would make starry the flowers and the grass. He
would have it that the world is but a shadow of
Blake's "Real and Eternal world": that we who
are shadows cling to the superstition that we are
not, and have but prejudiced and fearful ears for
his prophecies. He sees the world as a common-
wealth of angels and men and beasts and herbs;
and in it, horrible discords that we others scarcely
hear seem to him to strike the stars.

> Each outcry of the hunted hare
> A fibre from the brain doth tear;
> A skylark wounded on the wing
> Doth make a cherub cease to sing.

After all, in matters of the spirit, men are all
engaged in colloquies with themselves. Some of
them are overheard, and they are the poets. It is

his fortune that he is not overheard, at least by men.

Yet how much would he sacrifice could he but write a few verses in the old Welsh manner,—but a few verses like those he repeats as lovingly as others would their own. First, there is the elegy on Gwenhwyvar by Griffith ap Meredith ap Davydd:

The wearer of white and green, of red and blue,
Is now in the painful fold of death.
The Church conceals her—she whom velvet so adorned.
Wearer of velvet,
We mourn with tears now that the flush of her beauty has faded,
Now that the wearer of velvet and red is no more.

That he praises for its clear-eyed simplicity, its mournfulness direct as the cry of a child, as the bravery of this is as direct as the laughter of a child (it is by a poet who was also a prince):

I love the time of summer, when the charger
Of the exulting chief prances in the presence of a gallant lord,
When the nimbly moving wave is covered with foam,
When the apple tree is in flower,
And the white shield is borne on my shoulder to battle.

This, also, for its simple pride:

The men who went to Cattraeth were men of name:
Wine and mead out of gold was their drink:
Three men, and threescore, and three hundred, with golden
    torques.

How often will he repeat "with golden torques"!

But (and here some will reconsider their opinion that he is a fool, or one "not wise" as the pleasant Welsh phrase goes) there is no one that can laugh more loudly than he; or sing a song more happily; or join more lustily than he in hunting on foot, over the craggy hills, some fox which the farmer can never shoot when he comes for the turkeys in November; and in the heat of the run he will curse the hounds for gaining on the fox, and the fox for running no faster, saying that the worst of fox-hunting is that it is so one-sided, since the fox is not allowed to rejoice at the end with hounds and men.

And here is one of his imitative songs, reduced to its lowest terms by a translator:

> She is dead, Eluned,
> Whom the young men and the old men
> And the old women and even the young women
> Came to the gates in the village
> To see, because she walked as beautifully as a heifer.
>
> She is dead, Eluned,
> Who sang the new songs
> And the old; and made the new
> Seem old, and the old
> As if they were just born and she had christened them.
>
> She is dead, Eluned,
> Whom I admired and loved,
> When she was gathering red apples,

When she was making bread and cakes,
When she was smiling to herself alone and not thinking of me.

She is dead, Eluned,
Who was part of Spring,
And of blue Summer and red Autumn,
And made the Winter beloved;
She is dead, and these things come not again.

AZARIAH JOHN PUGH

One of the most inspiriting of our firesiders at the farmhouse is a young schoolmaster named Azariah John Pugh, and called, in the Welsh fashion, almost invariably, Azariah John.

He is mainly English and partly Spanish; he was born in England, but having a Welsh name, he boasts much of his country, as he has elected to call Wales. But in truth he belongs to no time or place. He cares nothing for the house he lives in, for the village, or for any place he ever saw. Yet are we never tired of hearing his rich sentiments about them all. If only he be far away from it, there is no place known to him which he will not magnify with words which others do not easily use even for their true loves. Probably he would like to like them; but that very liking seems to be due to his feverish wide reading in books that are full of sentiments he admires and would borrow, if he could. Thus, of old cities, rivers flowing past famous places, mountains of beauty or story, the white cliffs of the south, the whin-red moorland of Wales, old gardens, solemn woods, all solitudes, fading races, sunsets, fallen greatness in men and things, old books, old beer, poverty, childhood . . . of all these he will talk as if he had discovered them to the world, though it may be doubted whether he knows them at all. Yet is he a magnificent echo of the genuine lovers of these things, and he is so sorrowfully anxious to be believed that to some of us he has seemed to be the true heir, though defrauded of his inheritance, of all beauty and all antiquity. He is for ever speaking of "remembering afresh and with pleasure ancient matters," though he knows that even he cannot remember them with pleasure, and that no experienced man ever does so. He is so young that he has nothing to forget. But in his own esteem he is old now, and shakes his head over the light-heartedness of old men, saying, "If they were as old as I am——"

He speaks so suavely that the plain man wonders that he has never felt as deeply himself. Before his patriotism, the patriot is abashed. The lover of the quiet life, in his presence, is persuaded

that himself can hardly be said to love it. No
lover repeats more fondly—

> And I would send tales of forgotten love
> Late into the lone night, and sing wild songs
> Of maids deserted in the olden time.

He thus deceives every one but himself, and that
one exception is the real cause of his unhappiness.
He cannot avoid his affectations. He only finds
them out when they are full-grown and most noisily
and hungrily abroad in every man's ears, and then
he has to maintain them, wearily but with an
apparent gaiety. Pity even will not hurt him. It
is his genial air : he rejoices in it as a pigeon, leaning and raising her wing to expose her tender side,
rejoices in summer rain, and as languidly ; and then
again he is furious at it, and cultivates brutality,
drinks much beer, and uses many oaths, of which
he wearies and comes again to the old tap.

The ghosts of the subtle emotions which we say
make up modernity have come into his brain, and
they are so many that he has become, if not a
theatre, at least a mortuary, of modernity. But the
nervous strain of any real passion in his neighbourhood obliges him to be rude or to run away. Real
passion was always scandalously ill done : he would
have no lover die less romantically than Romeo.

And as his thoughts, so are his acts, except that they are few. He has been to Rome, the Bay of Spezzia, Windermere; he has walked along the Pilgrim's Road to Canterbury. He has learned to work badly in metal and wood. He has had whims and drugs enough to win an appreciation from Mr. Arthur Symons. He has written poems under the influence of something in his stomach; but either he cannot read them, or they are not fit to be read. He wrote one, I remember, about a girl who worked a story in tapestry while her lover played on a harp the melody which told the same story. He wrote a sermon on the death of John Jones because a hundred persons of that name die every day, and he wished to praise the average man, out of a whimsical distaste for his late less fantastic likings. He has had friends and has been left by them; or, as he says, after the Welsh poet,

The brave, the magnanimous, the amiable, the generous, and the
    energetic
Are as stepping-stones to the bard.

He has made love, and he has been scorned; the sad tunes of
                    Old unhappy far off-things
                    And battles long ago

are accordingly most dear to him, and in his gayest

moments he will murmur some sad melody like
"The Marsh of Rhuddlan" or "My Johnny was a
shoemaker." I have heard him repeat this strange
poem of Taliesin's as if he were a reincarnation of
the bard :

> Primary chief bard am I to Elphin,
> And my original country is the region of the summer stars ;
> Idno and Heinin called me Merddin,
> At length every King will call me Taliesin.
> I was with my Lord in the highest sphere,
> On the fall of Lucifer into the depth of hell ;
> I have borne a banner before Alexander ;
> I know the names of the stars from north to south. . . .
> I have been with my Lord in the manger of the ass ;
> I strengthened Moses through the water of Jordan ;
> I have been in the firmament with Mary Magdalene ;
> I have obtained the muse from the cauldron of Ceridwen ;
> I have been bard of the harp to Lleon of Lochlin ;
> I have been on the White Hill, in the court of Cynvelyn ;
> For a day and a year in stocks and fetters,
> I have suffered hunger for the Son of the Virgin.
> I have been fostered in the land of the Deity,
> I have been teacher to all intelligences,
> I am able to instruct the whole universe,
> I shall be until the day of doom on the face of the earth :
> And it is not known whether my body is flesh or fish. . . .

And it falls strangely from this wandering voice
that calls itself a man. It is comic and it is terrible.
He alone seems to feel the true sadness of them :
flatterers and low comic persons tell him that he is
but a vessel come into the world to be filled with

all the sorrows that have been. Truly, all that has passed, is.

Nevertheless, we love him for his gross natural self, for so we think his only convincing affectation, the only one which he displays with some consistency by the fireside ; and we know, as the world does not know, how costly and passionate affectations are.

Morgan Rhys and Others

I should like to win some charity for Morgan Rhys, the descendant of a prince, a bard and a tin-plater. Charity it must be ; for, in truth, he is something of a Celt in the bad, fashionable sense of that strange word, and is somewhat ridiculous beside the landlord of the " Cross Inn." An orphan, he lived as the only child in the large house of a distant relative, reading everything, playing half-heartedly at games, yet now and then entering into them with such enthusiasm that he did what he liked and won a singular reputation. He went seldom to a chapel, and when he went, did something more than escape boredom, by the marvellous gift of inattention which enabled him to continue his own chain of thought or fancy from beginning to end of the service. He was

quite unhindered by hymn, prayer, or sermon, and
accepted what he heard, as elderly persons accept
fairies, without even curiosity. The death of
others made him helpless for a time, but he did not
reason about the fact: his own death he at all
times contemplated without fear; what he feared,
if anything, was the fear of death.

These things would not be remarkable, if he had
not been at the same time an impressionable, sub-
missive child, incapable of listening to argument,
indeed, but of an unsatisfied sentimentality that
might have been made much use of by a priest.
His abstraction from things to which he was
indifferent was wonderful. He was delighted
and fascinated by abstraction itself, and finding a
thing uninteresting, he could at once withdraw
into a sweet, vaporous, empty cave. Thus, he
was praised at school for his calmness during
punishment, which, he says, on many occasions he
never felt at all.

When a child of five he had been left alone for
half a day in a remote chamber of a great house,
and at nightfall was found sitting at a window
that commanded an orchard and a lawn, and when
he did not rise to greet his friends, and was ques-
tioned, merely said "Look!" Nobody could see

anything, or rather, they saw everything as usual : nor could he explain. He always remembered the incident, and could not explain it. There was no fairy, no peculiar light or gloom. Yet he admitted that he was intoxicated by the mere trees and the green lawn. In the same way he was often found listening to silence. He did not pretend to hear strange music. It was the voluptuousness of sheer silence. At home, in the fields, at school, he would cry : " There ! " So far as any one could see, there was nothing. To shut his eyes was not to see amply and clearly, but to see infinite purple darkness, which he vastly loved. He would ask friends whether they remembered this place or that on a certain day, and if they did, could never have them share his pleasure at the recollection ; and for this whim he was scolded and ridiculed.

But at the age of sixteen or seventeen, poetry gave him a second world in which he thenceforward moved with a rapture which I do not often observe in the religious, while in religious matters he remains so pure a sceptic that he has never yet learned that there is anything about which to be sceptical. This so-called matter-of-factness in combination with a rich imaginativeness is perhaps a Welsh characteristic. I remember a

farmer in Cardiganshire, with the blood of a lamb
on his wrist, singing a fine hymn very nobly ; and
though I cannot like such a mystic, I admire him.
In the same way will Rhys turn from ribaldry to a
poem by Mr. Yeats. But he valued poetry not so
much because it was full of music for ear and
spirit, though that he loved ; not so much because
it was the first discoverer of Nature and Man,
though that he well knew, as because it revealed to
him the possibility of a state of mind and spirit in
which alone all things could be fully known at
their highest power, and that state was his most
cherished aim, and poetry helped him to achieve it.
Along with love of poetry went a curious study
of appearances and illusions. He was never tired
of considering them ; of trying to elucidate the
impressionism of the eyes and the other senses ;
of trying to know what there was in tree or face
or flower which many measurements, scientific
descriptions, photographs, and even pictures did
not exhaust. So many trees he saw were scarcely
more than nothing, though close by and in clear
air : what were they, he asked. He had never any
answer. "If only we could think like that !" he
said once, pointing to a fair, straight hawthorn
that stood, with few branches and without leaves,

on the mountain side. And he came to hope for
a state in which he and the trees and the great
estuary near his house, the flowers, the distant
white cottages, should become all happily arranged
in as perfect a pattern as that made with iron dust
by a magnet—all filling their places, all integral
parts of a whole, and important because they were.

One evening he came into the farmhouse in
deep excitement because (as he said) he had been
part of the music of the spheres. He had walked
through village after village, over the mountains
and along the rivers, under great motionless white
clouds. The air had been so clear that every straw
of the thatch gleamed separately. He had passed
through the lonely places with a sense of passing
through a crowd because the rich spring air had
been so much a presence. The men labouring or
idling in the fields had seemed to be seraphic and
majestic beings; the women smiling or talking by
the gates were solemn and splendid. When at
last he descended into this valley, he saw the wood
smoke rising gently and blue from all the houses,
as if they had been a peaceful company smoking
pipes together. He had looked at the sky, the
flushed mountain sheep, the little stony lanes
that led steeply up to farmyard and farm, the

jackdaw making suitable music high up in the cold bright air, the buzzard swirling amidst the young bracken, and he had approved, and had been approved, in ecstasy. And on that day the mazes of human activity had been woven into a rich pattern with the clouds and the hills and the waters for the pleasure of the gods, and were certainly for once fitted to the beauty and harmony of the universe. Thus he spoke in ejaculations, to our great joy, though not without giving us a fear that he would spoil it by something inapposite. But merely remarking that he had seen the parson feeding his boar and that the harmony between them also was complete, he became silent, and for a time the whole world shimmered and darkened as if it had been some tapestry which Rhys had made. The most pious member of the party, a Christian if ever there was one, remarked that he "wished he had felt like that sometimes." To which Rhys replied that he could not possibly wish that, as he would then be damned like himself: and the other agreed.

On days like this, he stepped over the edge of the world and saw the gods leaning from the stars among the clouds, and perhaps the loneliness that followed appalled him. For these days flew fast.

And so he tried to fortify himself by mingling
warmly with the life of every day in the village,
where his reputation was for generosity, hard drinking, and perfect latitude of speech. He stimulated
the trade-unionist, the parson, the minister, the
bard. But he could not live both lives. The
worldly one was the more difficult and he gave it
up, and only made spasmodic and gross attempts to
return to it. He began to shrink not only from all
men but from all outward experience, and to live, as
only too easily he could, upon his own fantasy. He
was "surprised" when he saw men in the street.
A million people, all different and their differences
so much the more difficult because they were not
acknowledged, frightened him. So his advocacy
of certain humane measures and his support of
some enthusiasms sounded as if they came from
an angel, a fiend, or a corpse. As will happen
with men who love life too passionately, he was
often in love with death. He found enjoyment in
silence, in darkness, in refraining from deeds, and
he longed even to embrace the absolute blank of
death, if only he could be just conscious of it; and
he envied the solitary tree on a bare plain high up
among the hills, under a night sky in winter where
the only touch of life and pleasure was the rain.

And now, with his fantastic belief that the corpse is life's handiwork and its utmost end, he is humanised only by a dread of the blank to which he is going :

> When we shall hear
> The rain and wind beat dark December, how,
> In that our pinching cave, shall we discourse
> The freezing hours away ?

He has made a heaven and he fears it.

Once there came to him and to the farmhouse a ghost from the north. He was a tall, black-haired, white-faced man, with high curved brow, straight fleshy nose, perfect firm lips, and bony chin. Was he soldier or scholar or priest ? asked one and another. His face was vigilant, of childlike freedom of expression, and yet of boundless mystery in repose. When he spoke, he had fire, dignity, rapidity, ease, fertility of ideas, and everything of the orator except that his speech was simple. He could move a Welsh multitude with politics as a wind moves the corn, yet he did so but once, because "it was a blackguard game." Distinguished from the rest only by his white tie, in the pulpit he looked a Loyola and was a Chrysostom ; yet he stood there but once or twice, to bury a noble man. He was master of an English style that was like Newman's in simplicity, music, and weight, yet published but

one pamphlet that was wrung from him by a needy
cause in a week, and never did anything to disabuse
a public that praised him for it. His handwriting,
in any haste, was that of a leisured and proud monk.
His deep voice had a kind of flame-like hum of
passion in it; he always used it in the service of the
beautiful and the true. I heard him laugh only
once, and then the depth which he discovered for
a moment disturbed me so that I distrusted all
laughter afterwards : it was like a nymph emerging
from a deep cave. In scorn, in ignorance, in mere
contentedness, he never uttered a word. He is
content to be the light and the rest of a few scholars
and a hundred miners, and to be the faithful, un-
honoured Levite of the mighty dead, of whom not
one, or prince or bard, had a virtue which he has
not, except it were a strong right arm and the will
to make a war in which to use it for the service
of the liberty and integrity of Wales, for these
alone of mortal things he passionately loves.

Lastly, there is at the farmhouse still a memory
of that poet, great discoverer of manuscripts and
splendid human being—Iolo Morganwg—also herb-
alist, lover of liberty and of the Revolution in
France, a mighty walker, who would ride in no man's
coach, and having been given a horse, drove it before

him for a long way, and complained that a horse
was wearisome. He learned his alphabet from the
tombstones which his father made. In his youth,
in the middle of the eighteenth century, he thought
of going to America to search for the Welsh colony
left five hundred years before by Madoc ap Owen
Gwynedd, whom Southey strove to sing. He was
stone-mason, bookseller, land-surveyor and (in slave-
owning days) seller of sugar "uncontaminated by
human gore." Eighty years ago he was to be seen
"on the highways and byways of Glamorgan—an
elderly pedestrian of rather low stature, wearing his
long grey hair flowing over his high coat-collar,
which by constant antagonism had pushed up his
hat brim into a quaint angle of elevation behind.
His countenance was marked by a combination of
quiet intelligence and quick sensitiveness; the
features angular, the lines deep, and the grey eye
benevolent but highly excitable. He was clad in
rustic garb: the coat blue, with goodly brass
buttons, and the nether integument good homely
corduroy. He wore buckles in his shoes, and a pair
of remarkably stout well-set legs were vouchers for
the great peripatetic powers he was well known to
possess. A pair of canvas wallets were slung over
his shoulders, one depending in front, the other

behind. These contained a change of linen and a few books and papers connected with his favourite pursuits " (the study and collection of old Welsh manuscripts for the illustration of Welsh history). " He generally read as he walked, ' with spectacles on nose,' and a pencil in his hand serving him to make notes as they suggested themselves. A tall staff, which he grasped at about the level of his ear, completed his travelling equipment." And in this chair, they say, he spent a night, sleeping and reading alternately.

Outside, by the window, is the village idiot, with a smile like the sound of bells ascending from a city buried in the sea.

CHAPTER V

January

I

THE road ran for ten miles between mountains on which the woods of oak and fir moaned, though there was little wind. A raven croaked with a fat voice. I could hear a score of streams. But the valley would not speak with me. The sole joy in it was that of walking fast and of seeing the summits of the hills continually writing a wild legend on the cloudy sky. The road curved and let in the poor sunlight from the south-west; and there were interminable oak woods ahead,—one moan and one dull cloud.

But, suddenly, a space of the south-west sky was silver white. The sun was almost visible, and, suddenly, a company of oak trees caught the light and shone, and became warm and glorious, but

misty and impenetrable with light.   They dreamed
of summers to come and summers past.   For one
moment they were as fine and strange and chosen
from all the rest, as things discovered by a lantern
on a country road at night.   Not only were they
impenetrable to the sight, but it was impossible
to suppose oneself amongst them.   They were
holding festival, but not for me.   They were
populous, but not with men.   They were warm
and welcoming, and something was happy there.
They were as a large, distant, and luminous house
seen in a cold and windy night by some one hungry,
poor, timid, and old, upon a lonely road, envying it
with an insatiable envy that never dreams of satisfying itself.

But, in a moment, a mist arose from the grass
between the oaks and me : the glory departed :
and the little, draughty farmhouse was far more
to be desired than they, where a soft-voiced motherly
girl of twenty gave me cheese and bread and milk,
and smiled gently at the folly of walking on such
a day.

II

All day I wandered over an immense, bare,
snowy mountain which had looked as round as a
white summer cloud, but was truly so pitted and

scarred and shattered by beds of streams and valleys full of rotten oak trees, that my course wound like a river's or like a mouse's in a dense hedge. The streams were small, and, partly frozen, partly covered up by snow, they made no noise. Nothing made any noise. There was a chimney-stack clearly visible ten miles away, and I wished that I could hear the factory hiss and groan. No wind stirred among the trees. Once a kite flew over among the clouds of the colour of young swan's plumage, but silently, silently. I passed the remains of twelve ancient oaks, like the litter of some uncouth, vast monster pasturing, but without a sound.

The ruins of a farm lay at the edge of one valley : snow choked the chimney and protected the hearth, which was black with flames long dead, and as cold as a cinerary urn of the bronze age. I stumbled over something snowy near by, and exposed the brown fragments of a plough, and farther on, a heavy wheel standing askew on its crumbling axle.

The trees below were naked on one side of their boles, but above was the snow, like a stiff upright mane on every branch, which seemed to have forced them into their wild and painful curves.

All the fallen rotten wood broke under my foot without a sound, and the green things disclosed were as some stupid, cheerful thing in a house of tremendous woe.

It was impossible to think of the inn to which I was going, and hardly of the one which I had left. How could their fires have survived the all-pervading silent snow? When one is comfortable, near a fire or within reach of one, and in company, winter is thought of as a time of activity, of glowing faces, of elements despised, and even a poetry book brings back the spring: one will run, or eat chestnuts, or read a book, or look at a picture to-morrow, and so the winter flies. But on the mountain there was no activity; it was impertinent: there was the snow. When I could remember anything it was these verses, which were the one survival from the world I had known before I began to cross this immense, bare, snowy mountain:

> The beams flash on
> And make appear the melancholy ruins
> Of cancelled cycles; anchors, beaks of ships;
> Planks turned to marble; quivers, helms and spears,
> And gorgon-headed targes, and the wheels
> Of scythéd chariots, and the emblazonry
> Of trophies, standards, and armorial beasts,
> Round which death laughed, sepulchred emblems
> Of dead destruction, ruin within ruin!

The wrecks beside of many a city vast,
Whose population which the earth grew over
Was mortal, but not human; see, they lie,
Their monstrous works, and uncouth skeletons,
Their statues, homes and fanes; prodigious shapes
Huddled in grey annihilation, split,
Jammed in the hard, black deep; and over these,
The anatomies of unknown winged things,
And fishes which were isles of living scale,
And serpents, bony chains, twisted around
The iron crags, or within heaps of dust
To which the tortuous strength of their last pangs
Had crushed the iron crags; and over these
The jagged alligator, and the might
Of earth-convulsing behemoth, which once
Were monarch beasts, and on the slimy shores,
And weed-overgrown continents of earth,
Increased and multiplied like summer worms
On an abandoned corpse, till the blue globe
Wrapped deluge round it like a cloke, and they
Yelled, gasped, and were abolished; or some God
Whose throne was in a comet, passed, and cried
Be not!

They lay beneath; the snow was over them. It was hard to walk while all things had thus, in Asiatic phrase, perfected their repose. When the distant chimney appeared again, it was as incredible as a thing seen in a dream when one knows that it is a dream. It interrupted the perfection of the whole, as I did, but only as the smell of a mouse may spoil the beauty of an old room which has been left for a dead man alone, for some time after the funeral. The farther I went, the more immense became the extent of hills ahead and around. Their whiteness made the sky gloomy, as if with coming night. The furthest were grey with distance. In the cold that overtook my swiftest walking I could not put by the imagination that I could see myself travelling over more endless white hills, lost, to my own knowledge, and yet beyond my own power to save. And, again, I thought of all the hills beyond those I saw, until even the immensity before me became more awful, because it suggested the whole, as the light of one candle by the organist suggests the whole cathedral at midnight.

And then, though I did not know it, a change began, and dimly, not hopefully, as when one thinks one hears the double click of a latch in a house which strangers inhabit now, I saw that the sun began to set, and it was red. I knew that red : it belonged to the old world : it was the colour of the oast houses in Kent. A window, two miles off, caught the light and blazed. A bell told the hour in a church, and shook some of the snow from the belfry in a mist. I warmed myself in the breath of a flock of sheep. I knew that I heard the voice of a stream which had been with me for a long

way. Borrow, I remembered, knew the stream.
Borrow! I was at home again.

Slowly the fire and the ale constructed the world
again, and though I could still see the snow from
the hearth of the inn, it was as impotent as the
frail moon which was convoyed down among the
moorlands by dark and angry clouds, while I read—
as now my reader does—this passage from *Wild
Wales* :—

"'I suppose you follow some pursuit besides
bardism?' said I; 'I suppose you farm?'

"'I do not farm,' said the man in grey. 'I keep
an inn.'

"'Keep an inn?' said I.

"'Yes,' said the man in grey. 'The —— Arms
at L——.'

"'Sure,' said I, 'inn-keeping and bardism are
not very cognate pursuits?'

"'You are wrong,' said the man in grey; 'I
believe the *awen*, or inspiration, is quite as much at
home at the bar as in the barn, perhaps more. It
is that belief which makes me tolerably satisfied
with my position and prevents me from asking Sir
Richard to give me a farm instead of an inn.'

"'I suppose,' said I, 'that Sir Richard is your
landlord?'

"'He is,' said the man in grey, 'and a right noble landlord too.'

"'I suppose,' said I, 'that he is right proud of his tenant?'

"'He is,' said the man in grey, 'and I am right proud of my landlord, and will here drink his health. I have often said that if I were not what I am, I should wish to be Sir Richard.'

"'You consider yourself his superior?' said I.

"'Of course,' said the man in grey; 'a baronet is a baronet, but a bard is a bard, you know. I never forget what I am, and the respect due to my sublime calling. About a month ago I was seated in an upper apartment, in a fit of rapture; there was a pen in my hand and paper before me on the table, and likewise a jug of good ale, for I always find that the *awen* is most prodigal of her favours when a jug of good ale is before me. All of a sudden my wife came running up and told me that Sir Richard was below, and wanted to speak to me. "Tell him to walk up," said I. "Are you mad?" said my wife. "Do you know who Sir Richard is?" "I do," said I; "a baronet is a baronet, but a bard is a bard. Tell him to walk up." Well, my wife went and told Sir Richard that I was writing and could not come down, and that she hoped he would not object to walk up. "Certainly not, certainly not," said Sir Richard. "I shall be only too happy to ascend to a genius on his hill. You may be proud of such a husband, Mrs. W." And here it will be as well to tell you that my name is W.—J. W. of ——. Sir Richard then came up, and I received him with gravity and politeness. I did not rise, of course, for I never forget myself a moment, but I told him to sit down, and added, that after I had finished the *pennill* (song for the harp) I was engaged upon, I would speak to him. Well, Sir Richard smiled and sat down, and begged me not to hurry myself, for that he could wait. So I finished the *pennill*, deliberately, mind you, for I did not forget who I was, and then turning to Sir Richard, entered upon business with him.'

" 'I suppose Sir Richard is a very good-tempered man ?' said I.

" 'I don't know,' said the man in grey. 'I have seen Sir Richard in a devil of a passion, but never with me. No, no! trust Sir Richard for not riding the high horse with me. A baronet is a baronet, but a bard is a bard, and that Sir Richard knows.' "

The which Borrovianism should as much delight

my hard-working reader as it did me, on that
January night : may it console him also.

February

I

I passed through a village where I found
that the old-fashioned bidding marriage was not
dead. For a printed sheet with this announcement
(in Welsh) fell into my hands :

A BIDDING TO A MARRIAGE

Inasmuch as we intend entering the
state of wedlock on ——, we invite
wedding gifts, which will be repaid
with thanks on a like occasion.

T. Williams.
Elizabeth Jones.

It is expected that gifts due to them,
and to their parents and brothers,
will be paid on the wedding day.

The custom was old ; the village was new, and
it stood on the edge of a strange new land. Having
passed it, the road dipped among sublime black hills
of refuse from furnace and pit. The streams were
rich with yellow water, purple water. Here and

there were dim, shining, poisonous heaps of green
and blue, like precious stones. There were railway
lines everywhere, and on them trucks, full of scraps
of metal, like sheaves of scimitars and other cruel
weapons—still cruel, but hacked, often rusty, and
expressing something more horrible than mere
sharpness and ferocity. There were furnaces,
crimson and gold; and beyond all, a white-clouded
sky which said that it was over the sea.

In the early afternoon a grey mist invested all
things, so that even when I was close to them,
they seemed about to pass away, and I was tempted
to walk regardless and straight ahead as the harper
did in the tale.

It is told that a harper was asked to play and
sing at a wedding. It was a fine day, and on his
way he sometimes played over the melodies he most
liked; and as he went, the fairies followed him,
their little feet going fast and sharp like drumsticks.
When he reached the house, the fairies were still
behind him. They followed him in, and presently,
since he again tuned his harp, the company began
to dance, and the fairies with them; the house,
which was a little one, did not impede them;
and in no long time they all went dancing out of
the house. The fairies, it is said, were not to be

distinguished from the bridal party. They went on across well-known country, regardless and straight ahead, through a barn where men were threshing, through a hall where men were dining. Coming at last to a place he did not know, the harper ceased and became separated from the rest, and slept. When he awoke, he found himself in a pleasant place among very little people, and all that was asked of him was that he should play on the harp every night. Then one day he got leave to go out of the land of the fairies; but he left his harp there and could never get back again. He found that the others had returned. He could say nothing of the wedding day, except that he had never before harped so well.

And well did the mist harp. It was the one real credible thing among those furnaces, which were but as gaps in it, or as landscapes seen rapidly from small windows in a lofty house upon a hill.

II

Next day I crossed the river. At first, the water seemed as calm and still as ice. The boats at anchor, and doubled by shadow, were as if by miracle suspended in the water. No ripple was to be seen, though now and then one emitted a

sudden transitory flame, reflected from the sun,
which dreamed half-way up the sky in a cocoon of
cloud. No motion of the tide was visible, though
the shadows of the bridge that cleared the river in
three long leaps, trembled and were ever about to
pass away. The end of the last leap was unseen,
for the further shore was lost in mist, and a solitary
gull spoke for the mist. A sombre, satanic family
of what had yesterday been the chimneys of
factories rose out of the mist,—belonging to a
remote, unexplored, inaccessible country over there,
which seemed to threaten the river-side where I
stood. But the tide was rising, and the thin long
wavering line of water grew up over the mud, and
died, and grew up again, curved like the grain of
a chestnut or mother-of-pearl, and fascinating,
persuasive. And sometimes the line of water
resembled a lip, quivering with speech, and yet
silent, unheard. Two swans glimmered at the
edge; and beneath them, in the water, and beside
them, on the polished mud, their white reflections
glimmered.

Suddenly the tantara of a trumpet stung me
like an enormous invisible wasp, and I looked
down and saw a grey, drowned dog at my feet.
His legs lay in pairs; his head curved towards his

fore-legs, his tail towards his hind-legs. He was of
the colour of the mud. But his very quietness
and powerlessness and abjectness, without any consideration of all the play and strife and exercise
that once led him step by step towards death,—
without a thought of the crimson tongue that once
flickered, after hunting or fighting, like a flame
of pure abandoned vitality,—gave me a strange
suggestion of power and restraint, just as the misty
land over the water, without any consideration of
all the men and machinery that were visible there
yesterday, suggested a life without those things.
The beast became a puissant part of the host of
all the dead or motionless or dreaming things, of
statuary and trees and dead or inefficient men, and
was, with them, about to convince me of a state
quite other than ours, and not worse, when once
again the trumpet disturbed me and turned me to
the thought that I was the supreme life-giver to
these things, that I gave them of myself, and that
without me they were nothing; and I feared that
this fancied state was but suggested by my envy
of calm things, and that, though dreams may put
the uttermost parts of the earth into our possession,
without the dream the dreamer is nothing more
than naught.

III

Thence I went to an irregular, squalid, hideous, ashen town,—a large village, but noisy and without character, neither English nor Welsh. The street songs were but a week or two behind those of London, and they were not mixed with anything but an occasional Welsh hymn tune or "Sospan bach." But there used to be an old house there that spoke of old Wales, and I went to see it.

When I came to the edge of its garden I heard a blackbird sing, and in the busy street how old and far away it sounded! as if it were true that "thrice the age of a man is that of a stag, and thrice that of a stag is that of the melodious blackbird."

Pretentious, unpicturesque, fatigued, and silent, the women walked to and fro, between the shops. Now and then an unmarried girl laughed; the others had no such energy.

It was more pleasant to be among the men, who were on the other side of the road, many of them standing still, packed close in a half-moon figure that swelled out over the pavement, and watching something. There was nothing gorgeous or adventurous or even elegant in their scrupulous dress;

in the old faces either alcoholic or parched, in the waxen faces of the younger; in the voices which seemed to have been copied from the gramophone, their favourite instrument. I liked them for the complete lack of self-consciousness which allowed them to expose quite fearlessly their angular figures, their uninteresting clothes, their heartless, rigid faces that retained smiles for an incredibly short time. They were the equals, in everything but ease, of the labourers whom they were watching. But when I saw at last what they were watching, I thought that I could have rejoiced to have seen them, looking passionate for once, in flames.

For, under the direction of a foreman, whose snub nose, bow legs, and double collar made him a sublime and monstrous priest or chief of what was most horrible among the men and women of the street, a band of labourers, without pity, without even ferocity, but mechanically, was demolishing "Quebec," a dignified mid - eighteenth - century house, where for five generations a decent, stable professional family had lived, loved beauty according to its lights, and been graceful in its leisure. The very house had seemed to say, amid its troubled neighbours, as Marlowe's Edward said,

This life contemplative is heaven.

Now it was falling in thunders and clouds of ruin; and I wondered that the people did not fall upon the enormous, red-haired, passionless men who wielded the pickaxes.

For twenty years I had known "Quebec" and had watched the streets creeping upon it, until the house and great garden were surrounded and spied upon by houses on all sides but one. That one side had been protected by a lofty and massive wall, and through that the enemy had now broken an entrance.

Behind that wall, the two Alderneys had grazed on three acres of meadow, in the midst of which had been an old orchard, and in the midst of that the gardens and the house. Once I had seen a girl with the delicate Kentish rake gathering a little hay there. In one corner, too, had been a tangle of elder and bramble, which (so we used to fancy) might possibly have—by pure and unbroken descent, miraculously escaping all change—the sap of Eden in their veins.

But the Alderneys were gone, and the meadow was slashed with ruts; the trees were down; the air was foul with dust of mortar and brick and plaster; and, mocking at the disembowelled house, new bricks, scaffolding, and iron pillars and girders lay round about, among the fallen clouds of ivy, which were torn and dead. Oh, Westminster, Tintern, Godstow, Kidwelly, you have immortality, not indeed in your forms, but in the hearts of men; but "Quebec" dies with me! So I thought and wondered.

Hastily broken up, without a grave, without ceremonial, without a becoming interval of desolation in which to spend its tears, and have at least the pleasure of regret, the house, I knew, could not but send forth piteous ghosts to wander up and down,—*inops, inhumataque turba*,—and round their heads garlands of branches with those terrible buds that were never to be leaves,—until their sorrows and ours were smoothed by time or consumed by death. I met them afterwards in spring, when the purple of the brambles should have been at last overcome by green, and they seemed the sole inhabitants of the brand-new, crowded streets, beneath which "Quebec" is buried.

Suddenly I met Philaster, who had years ago rung the great bell of the house and become the angry coachman's willing captive, so that he might see the house quite close, and the flowers and the grass. Between us we made the power of the breaker and builder as naught. For a little while, indeed, we asked, What would other children do who lived in that suburb, and had no "Quebec" to provide a home for all their fancies,—to lend its lawns for bright ladies and brave knights to walk upon,—its borders and bowers to complete the scenery of Hans Andersen,—its grey walls to hide beauty and cruelty, misers and witches, and children crying because of wicked stepmothers? We had set out, as children, to live as if for eternity. Now we would live as if for annihilation to-morrow. We would no longer set our hearts upon anything which the world can destroy. We would set our hearts upon things of the imagination—like "Quebec."

So we went up into an attic, and drew the curtains, and lit the fire, and took draughts of long oblivion, and made our sorrows pompous by reading Villon and Catullus and Du Bellay, and the close of *Paradise Lost*, and the thirteenth book of the *Morte Darthur*, and Goethe's " Now comes first love and friendship's company," and other things that reminded us of decay and beauty ; and not one of them but drew a long echo from the hoary walls of "Quebec" (now safe within our brains). Yet not one of these things, however splendid or tumultuous or tender, was then too splendid or tumultuous or tender for our mood. Nor could one of them stir

us so potently as the picture that came often that
evening to our minds.   Here was the gaudy, dismal,
roaring street, its roar sometimes settling into
a kind of silence through which the heart longs
for voice of woman or bird to penetrate; and
there, seen over the high wall, was the old man
who owned "Quebec," playing bowls with several
happy children in the twilight, and half-hidden
by the dense border of hollyhock, red-hot poker,
blush roses, nasturtium, and sunflower; and the
house itself, looking more distant than it was,
in that sweet light, seemed to possess those
calm, impregnable high places of the wise, than
which, says Lucretius, there is no possession
more desirable.

March

I

Just before dawn, I came to a cleft high in
the hills, so that I could only see a little copse of
oak and hazel, and in the dying moonlight a
thousand white islands of cloud and mountain

Totus conlucens veste atque insignibus albis.

The night had gone, and the day had not come;
and the little copse had the serious, brooding air

which all things have at that hour, and especially
when the land is tender with the first hope of spring
and in that reverie—

Cette rêverie
Que ne pense à rien.

For what I saw seemed but the fragments of something which night had built for its own delight, and
as they became clearer and clearer they had more
and more the appearance of being unbuilt and
dissolved. But, gradually, the birds were let out
and they sang. Their songs, on the wintry hill,
which I had last visited in summer, broke upon
the silence as in summer they never do, like the
opening of the door of a room that is empty but
has once been gay with fire and books and men;
and sweet though the blackbird was, and shrill the
missel - thrush, their songs were awful, and said
that "a large part of the earth is still in the
urn unto us." The grass, which had truly been
of no colour, though my urgent memory persuaded me that it was green, began to awake to
colour, and, while in the shadow of the copse
the dusk was impenetrable, the light reached
a knoll where there was dead bracken still.
"Colour," said Novalis, "is an effort of matter to
become light," and for one moment the grass

upon that knoll ceased to strive and was light. A plover that wheeled close by disappeared and was but a glow.

I went on, and on a lower slope the ploughman was beginning to plough in the shadow. Grim and worthless looked the work, until I looked round and saw the dawn that was being prepared. But I watched too carefully, for I saw it all. Ever, as it grew, statelier and richer, I said to myself, that in a little while it would be perfected: yet still I watched and I began to think of those who saw it, as I had seen it before, from windows of towns, as they rose for work, or as they douted the candles and put away cards or books, and paused for perhaps a minute, and gazed as they never gazed at human beauty, because, though they revered it, they feared it also, and though they feared it they were fascinated. I thought of those that leapt up at it; those that mourned because they had seen it pass so often before into a common day; those that, on inhospitable roads, saw it and neglected it, or cursed it after a night in which they had drunk their last poor earnings altogether. If it would but last . . . I had been looking at it and had not seen it, and when I dropped these thoughts I knew that it was gone, the slowly prepared and solemn dawn which made the splendid spring of that year.

II

Then I took a path which led out of sight of the white crested mountain and down among larches and oaks.

The wind was changing the grass from green to silver, and back again, rhythmically. In the pallid herbage at the edge of the wood it produced many little sounds, the combination of them barely louder than the sound which fancy makes among tombs ; and yet that little concert passed into the ear and heart, giving a sympathy with the thousand minute sorrows of the inanimate world and a feeling that is part of the melancholy so importunately intruding on a spring day. But there, too, was trefoil, delicatest herbage of the early year, with its trick of globing and preserving rain upon its foliage, so that it is more delicate still in the grey dawn. One stalk with all its leaf singularly fine and small had grown out of a scar in a teazel stem.

So I came into a valley, and there was one white house in it, with a green, glowing, and humming garden, and at the door a woman who might have been the Old Year. It was one of those white houses so fair that in the old time a poet compared a girl's complexion with them, as with lilies and foam. It held all the sun, so that suddenly I knew that in another valley, farther south and farther east, the rooks were making the lanes sleepy with their busy talk; the kingfishers were in pairs on the brooks, whose gentle water was waving and combing the hair of the river moss; the gold of the willow catkin was darkened by bees; over an old root of dock was a heaving colony of gleaming ants; perhaps the chiffchaff had come to the larches and the little green moschatel was in flower with large primroses among the ash stoles in wet woods; and in the splendid moments of the day the poplars seemed to come into the world, suddenly, all purple. . . .

Yet here there was no rich high-hedged lane, no poplar, no noise of rooks, but only a desolate brown moorland crossed by deep swift brooks through which the one footpath ran, and this white house, like a flower on a grave, recalling these memories of other valleys; so that I forgot that near by the birches stood each in a basin of foam from the dripping of mist and rain, and that I had not yet seen a thrush's nest in any hawthorn on those hills. Therefore, I counted that house as lucky for me as the Welshman's hazel-stick in the tale that is told in Iolo Morganwg's life.

This is the tale.

A Welshman, with a fine hazel-stick in his hand, was once stopped on London Bridge by an Englishman, who asked whence he came. "From my own country," said the Welshman churlishly. "Do not take it amiss," said the Englishman; "and if you will tell me what I ask, and take my advice, it will be much for your good. Under the roots of the tree from which came your stick, there are great treasures of gold and silver; if you can remember the place, and will take me to it, I will make the treasure yours."

Now knowing that the fellow was a magician, the Welshman, though at first unwilling to be a party in this strange thing, at length agreed, and went with him to Craig-y-Dinas and showed him the hazel-tree. They dug out the root and found a broad flat stone underneath, which covered the entrance to a cave. They went in, the magician warning the Welshman lest he should touch a bell that hung in the middle of their path. At the spacious further end of the cave, they saw many warriors lying asleep in a circle, with bright armour on, and weapons ready at hand. One of the warriors, refulgent above all the rest, had a jewelled and golden crown along with the shield and battle-axe at his side.

At the feet of the warriors, in the middle of the circle, they saw two immense heaps, the one of gold, the other of silver, and the magician told the Welshman that he might take away as much as he could carry from either of the heaps. So he took much gold. The magician took nothing. On their way out of the cave he again warned the Welshman lest he should touch the bell. But should he touch it, said the magician, some of the warriors would surely awake and ask "if it was yet day": to which he must at once answer: "No, sleep thou on," whereupon the warriors would sleep again. And this the Welshman found to be truth when he staggered under his gold and grazed the bell; but remembering the other's words, he said: "Sleep thou on" when the warriors asked if it were day; and they slept.

When they had left the cave, and closed the entrance, the magician told the Welshman that he might return to the cave whenever he wished; that the warriors were the knights of King Arthur, and the warrior with the jewelled and golden crown was King Arthur; that they were awaiting

the day when the Black Eagle and the Golden
Eagle should go to war; for on that day the
trembling earth would toll the bell, and at that
sound the king and the knights of the king would
awake, take their weapons, overthrow the Saxon,
recover the island of Britain, and again establish
their king at Caerlleon, in justice and in peace and
for ever. But the Welshman spent his gold. He
went again to the cave; he overloaded his back
with gold; he stumbled and the bell rang; he
forgot the password. And the knights rose and
leaned upon their elbows, and one of them stood
up and took away his gold and beat him and thrust
him out and closed the mouth of the cave; and
though he and many others made all the hill sore
with their digging, the cave was not found again.

April

I

For half a day there was now a world of snow,
a myriad flakes falling, a myriad rising, and nothing
more save the sound of rivers; and now a world of
green undulating hills that smiled in the lap of the
grey mountains, over which moved large clouds,
sometimes tumultuous and grey, sometimes white

and slow, but always fringed with fire. When the snow came, the mountains dissolved and were not. When the mountains were born again out of the snow, the snow seemed but to have polished the grass, and put a sharper sweetness in the song of the thrush and the call of the curlew, and left the thinnest of cirrus clouds upon the bare field, where it clung only to the weeds. So, in this dialogue of mountain and snow, nothing was easily remembered or even credible, until I came to the foot of a hill which hazels and oak trees crowned. The snow was disappearing and the light came precipitately through it and struck the hill. All the olive and silver and leaden stems of oak and hazel glowed together and made a warm haze and changed the hill into an early sunset cloud out of which came the cooing of wood-pigeons. The mountains lay round, grey, faint, unimportant, about to pass away; the country that lay between them and the hill was still in mist. So the hill rose up crowned and garlanded like a statue in a great hall of some fair woman of whom one wonders what art can persuade her to stay on that cold pedestal for ever. The wood-pigeons cooed continually; and there was the hill, using all the sunlight, as a chrysanthemum will do in a London street. It lived; it appealed to all the sense and brain together; it was splendid; it was Spring's, and I do not know of anything else that mattered or was, for the time. Very sweet it was to see the world as but a shining green hill and a shining brown wood, with a wood-pigeon for a voice, while all other things that had been were gone like the snow. That there was also a wind I knew only because it brought with it the scent of a farmyard behind: for it had motion but no sound. Something in me was content to see the hill as a monument of Spring that might endure for ever, that the wood-pigeons might coo their song; and saw that it made possible the sound of bells in an evening landscape, of wheat in sheaves, and quiet beeches and doves among them. Yet I climbed to the wood, and saw that last year's leaves were too thick yet for a flower to pierce them; and that same wind had found a brittle, dead ash-tree in which to sing a cold November song; and the pigeons clapped their wings and flew away. And that cold November song made me remember against myself the old legend of the child who played with fairies, but came once with her mother and saw them no more.

There were, says the story, at a small harbour belonging to Nefyn, some houses in which several families formerly lived; the houses are there still, but nobody lives in them now. There was one family there to which a little girl belonged; they used to lose her for hours every day; so her mother was very angry with her for being so much away. "I must know," said she, "where you go for your play." The girl answered that it was to Pin-y-Wig, "The Wig point," which means a place to the west of the Nefyn headland; it was there, she said, she played with many children. "They are very nice children,—much nicer," said the child, "than I am." "I must know whose children they are," was the reply; and one day the mother went with her little girl to see the children. It was a distance of about a quarter of a mile to Pin-y-Wig, and after climbing the slope and walking a little along the top they came in sight of the Pin. It is from this Pin that the people of Pen-yr-Allt got water, and it is from there they get it still. Now after coming near the Pin the little girl raised her hands with joy at the sight of the children. "Oh, mother," said she, "their father is with them to-day; he is not with them always; it is only some-times that he is." The mother asked the child where she saw them. "There they are, mother, running down to the Pin, with their father sitting down." "I see nobody, my child," was the reply, and great fear came upon the mother; she took hold of the child's hand in terror, and it came to her mind at once that they were the *Tylwyth Teg*. Never afterwards was the little girl allowed to go to Pin-y-Wig: the mother had heard that the Tylwyth Teg exchanged people's children with their own.

II

Yesterday, the flower of the wood-sorrel and the song of the willow-wren came together into the oak woods, and higher up on the mountain, though they were still grey, the larches were misty and it was clearly known that soon they would be green. The air was full of the bleating of lambs, and though there was a corpse here and there, so fresh and blameless was it that it hardly spoiled the day. The night was one of calm and breathing darkness; nor was there any moon; and therefore the sorrowful darkness and angularity of early spring valleys by moonlight, when they have no masses of foliage to make use of the beams, did not exist. It was dark and warm, and from the invisible orchard, where snow yet lay under the stone wall, came a fragrance which, though it was not May, brought into our minds the song that was made for May in another orchard high among hills:

Have you ne'er waked in the grey of the day-dawn
Whitely to stand at the window scarce seen,
Over the garden to peer in the May-dawn
Past to the fruit-close whose pale boughs not green
Slowly reveal a fresh faintness a-flutter
White to the young grass and pink to the sky?
O, then a low call to waking we utter:
"Bluth, lasses, apple-bluth spirts low and high."

Out, lasses, out, to the apple-garth hasten—
Nay, never tarry to net your glad hair—
Here are no lovers your kissed shoes to fasten
(O, for the days when girls' feet may go bare).
O'er the dim lawn the may-rime yet lingers,
Pallid and dark as the down of the dawn—
Gather your skirts in your delicate fingers,
Stoop as you run o'er the almond-hung lawn.

Look through the trees ere dawn's twilight is over—
Lo, how the light boughs seem lost in the stars;
Everywhere bluth the grey sky seems to cover
Quivering and scented, new spring's kisses' scars.
Wet are the blossoms to wash your faint faces—
Bury your faces cheek-deep in their chill;
Press the flushed petals and open your dresses—
So—let them trickle your young breasts to thrill.

Winter has wronged us of sunlight and sweetness,
We who so soon must be hid from the sun;
Winter is on us as summer's completeness
Faint-hearted drops down a tired world undone;
Brief is the bloom-time as sleepy maids' laughter
Who know not one bed-time 'tis summer's last day,
Though from the heart of the rose they have quaffed her.
Come, lasses, come, ere our rose world falls grey.

We had talked long into the night, and then as sleep came, out of this darkness peered the early timorous warble of a blackbird, and gradually all the birds in orchard, hedge, and wood made a thick mist or curtain of innumerable and indistinguishable notes through which still crept the bolder note of that same nearest blackbird. As the night lost its heaviness, though not its stillness, the continuous mist of songs grew thicker and seemed to produce or to be one with the faint darkness which so soon was to be light. It seemed also to be making the landscape which I saw being made, when I looked out. There, was the side of the hill; there the larches, the dark hedges, and the lingering snow and the orchard: they were what I had seen before, but changed and increased; and very subtle, plaintive, menacing, vast, was the work, though when the light had fully come, once more the larches, the hedges, and the orchard were as if they had never been sung to a new order of beauty by the mist of songs, and yet not the same, any more than a full coffin is the same as the lips and eyes and hands and hair, of which it contains all that we did not love. And still there were many songs; but you could tell who sung each of them, if you wished.

III

At the end of the month, when already the cuckoo had come and the blackthorn flowers among hawthorn branches were deceiving those who desired May, I went again to the hill where the wood-pigeons had cooed. I sat in a room in sight of it, during a cloud-gathering sunset. The white houses, which had earlier been like remnants of winter snow, were now like flowers. They and the misty larches and the birches gave a nuptial splendour to the old hills. Once more the land stood in preparation, as it stands year after year, so that one might think it expected a new dynasty of gods to come on May day, as often happened in the old time. And in the oaks and hazels the wood-pigeons cooed again. But when the sunset was perfect, they ceased as if they also feared and loved the white and green lines of cloud that lay over the hills—of a white and green which I had only seen together before in a crimpled, tender cabbage cut in two and lying half in bright water for the cook. Then the silence grew and grew, exciting and paining and pleasing and never satisfying the ear; so that I knew not whether the silence or the speech that preceded it was the more mysterious. For him that has ears there is nothing more expressive than speech ; but it is never unequivocal as silence is. The two are perhaps handmaidens to one another and inseparable parts in the universal harmony, although Maeterlinck says that a silent child is wiser than Plato eloquent.

A cuckoo had been singing, but now I heard it not ; no longer did the yellow-ammer insist, the thrush gossip, the blackbird muse ; the sounds of the house were dead : and I saw a hundred cows, some lying down, some moving so lazily— like sailing ships on a wide sea—that I could not see the changing of their pattern on the grass, and I was entangled in the unfathomable dream of the unending hills and the unending valleys.

In the room hung a landscape of savage hills, cloven by dark shadows and bright streams, and the glass reflected the calm grass and the hill and the oak and hazel woods which thus mingled with the picture at times and made a strange palimpsest of winter and spring. Now one and now the other predominated, until some one came in, as three cuckoos flew crying overhead, and sang this song, which gave the victory to spring :—

THE MAIDS OF CAERMARTHENSHIRE

And something like these were the Welsh words, which were by Watcyn Wyn:

Song and the harp desire to raise
To sweet Wales praise for its women;
Lads and their hearts have not one theme
So dear, no dream so clinging;
There are no maidens in the land
Like the maiden band of Caermarthen. . . .

Of modest looks and nimble feet,
They are just as fleet as the wind's wings;
Dearly and lovesomely each floats
Red petticoats out farther;
They dance it swiftly through the earth,
The maids who had birth in Caermarthen. . . .

When men would love they desire the way
Of these; for, I say it in earnest,
One is worth two or even three
Of the usual free brave women.
If I take a wife I shall kiss the braids
Of one of the maids of Caermarthen.

May

I

All the morning I had walked among the mountains, and snow had fallen; but gradually I descended, and found a hawthorn standing all white and alone; and, at first, the delicacy of the country had an air of unreality, as if it were but a fancy provoked by the grim, steep, cold heights. Nor, at first, were the small farmhouses quite so real as the crags I remembered. As I approached them, I seemed to be revisiting lands that belonged to a fictitious golden past; but as I came up to them, I was not undeceived, as I should have expected to be. How sweet and grave were the young larches! The brooks were not running as I had heard them up among the hills, but as brooks would run if I read of them at home and at ease in the verses of some tender poet, or as they will when I remember them many years hence. The sound of the world was heard only as the laughter of youthful voices

by the trout pools, or again as the pealing of bells
that presently grew and swelled and bubbled until
the valley in which they pealed overflowed with
the sound, and the moment of their ceasing was
not marked. So at last I gave up some of the
pleasure of sight and hearing and smell under the
influence of those very senses. For a fancy came of
a kind that is not easily avoided when spring and
our readiness for it come together. And the fancy
was that I was coming into a land whither had
fled the transient desirable things of childhood
and early youth. Especially was it the land to
which had fled the acquaintances of that time, who
were known, perhaps, only for one day—one spring
—with whom intimacy began to flower, and then
death or some less perfect destroyer intervened and
"slit the thin-spun life" and gave an unwithered
rose into our keeping—the memory of a laugh, a
revelation, a catch of fish. We did not know them
long enough to have doubts, self-questionings, the
egotistical indulgences in letters and conversations
of which we sometimes drink so deep that we taste
the lees and know futility. Or they passed away
as childish games do : we made an appointment
and never kept it, and so we never knuckled the
marble or saw the child again. We knew them

once, golden-haired, and with laughter which no
sigh followed, with clear voices in anger or love.
These grow not old! And with them are some of
those who were once as they, the friends who were
once acquaintances: for who does not pleasantly
(or bitterly) remember the first fresh moments
when, like a first glass, our friends, with all their
best qualities perhaps unknown, were tasted carelessly, the palate quite unsoiled and in no need of
the olives of charity; or the moments when, with
tastes and aims not yet mutually discovered, we
were yet dimly conscious of the end, seeing the
whole future under vague light? Some of these
we can—and I did—recall as if the happy voices
had not died, but had simply made way for harsher
or sadder tones, and had fled here to keep an
immortality. I heard them on the fresh warm
air. And with them hovered those I saw but once
—in a crowd, at a wayside inn—and desired; and
at my evening inn some empty chairs were not
wholly in vain. Thus did the shadow of the
mountain fall far over the soft lands below.

II

All sign of snow had left the hills, when
long before sunrise, but not before the east had

begun to grow serious with thoughts of dawn, I
came upon a rough meadow, where a solitary thorn
was white with flower—or of that colour which
white is in the dusk. It reminded me of snow,
but prettily defying the mountains, it meant all
May. And it happened that the day then being
born was perfect May. The east opened, and the
close-packed, dwarfed hills were driven out of it
like sheep, into the gradual light. From that
moment until the day passed in a drift of purple
and dim cloud, all things were marvellously clear.
In the hedges, on the rough meadows, and in the
steep wastes under the cliffs, there were hundreds
of hawthorns flowering, and yet they were not
hundreds, but one and one and one. . . . They
were as a crowd of which we know all the faces,
and therefore no crowd at all; and one by one
these were to be saluted. Not only the white
thorns, but the oaks in the large fields, and even the
ashes and alders by the brooks were each distinct.
If I had raised my head, I should have seen, indeed,
that the mountains were in haze, and that what I
had just passed was in haze. But I never saw, or
wished to see, for more than a quarter of a mile,
and within that distance all things were clear and
separate, like books which oneself has handled and

known, every one. Even the daffodils under a
hazel hedge never became a patch. The women,
at gateways or among the cows, stood out like one
or two statues in a large vacant hall. One field
had in it twelve isolated oak trees, and that they
were twelve I saw clearly, and wondered and
admired, and never dreamed of thinking of them as
just a number of oaks. One by one the footpaths,
to left or right, went up to one of the oaks or
thorns, and, untrodden, disappeared suddenly. And
I could not but recall the lovely clear pictures in
old Welsh poetry and story which had on winter
nights reminded me of May. And chiefly this,
from the *Mabinogion*, was in my mind.

"'I was,' said Kynon, 'the only son of my
mother and father, and I was exceedingly aspiring,
and my daring was very great. I thought there
was no enterprise in the world too mighty for me,
and after I had achieved all the adventures that
were in my own country, I equipped myself and
set forth through deserts and distant regions. And
at length it chanced that I came to the fairest
valley in the world, wherein were trees of equal
growth ; and a river ran through the valley, and a
path was by the side of the river. And I followed
the path until mid-day, and continued my journey

along the remainder of the valley until the evening; and at the extremity of a plain I came to a large and lustrous castle, at the foot of which was a torrent. And I approached the castle, and there I beheld two youths with yellow curling hair, each with a frontlet of gold upon his head, and clad in a garment of yellow satin, and they had gold clasps upon their insteps. In the hand of each of them was an ivory bow, strung with the sinews of the stag; and their arrows had shafts of the bone of the whale, and were winged with peacock's feathers; the shafts also had golden heads. And they had daggers with blades of gold, and with hilts of the bone of the whale. And they were shooting their daggers.

"'And a little way from them I saw a man in the prime of life, with his beard newly shorn, clad in a robe and a mantle of yellow satin; and round the top of his mantle was a band of gold lace. On his feet were shoes of variegated leather, fastened by two bosses of gold. When I saw him, I went towards him and saluted him, and such was his courtesy that he no sooner received my greeting than he returned it. And he went with me towards the castle. Now there were no dwellers in the castle except those who were in one hall. And there I saw four-and-twenty damsels, embroidering satin at a window. And this I tell thee, Kai, that the least fair of them was fairer than the fairest maid thou hast ever beheld in the Island of Britain, and the least lovely of them was more lovely than Gwenhwyvar, the wife of Arthur, when she has appeared loveliest at the Offering, or on the day of the Nativity, or at the feast of Easter. They rose up at my coming, and six of them took my horse, and divested me of my armour; and six others took my arms, and washed them in a vessel until they were perfectly bright. And the third six spread cloths upon the tables and prepared meat. And the fourth six took off my soiled garments, and placed others upon me; namely, an under vest and a doublet of fine linen, and a robe, and a surcoat, and a mantle of yellow satin with a broad gold band upon the mantle. And they placed cushions both beneath and around me, with coverings of red linen; and I sat down. Now the six maidens who had taken my horse unharnessed him, as well as if they had been the best squires in the Island of Britain. Then, behold, they brought bowls of silver wherein was water to wash, and towels of linen, some green and some white; and I washed. And in a little while the man sat down to the table. And I sat next to him, and below me sat all the maidens, except those who waited on us. And the table was of silver, and the cloths upon the table were of linen; and no vessel was served upon the table that was not either of gold or of silver or of buffalo horn. And our meat was brought to us. And, verily, Kai, I saw there every sort of meat and every sort of liquor that I have ever seen elsewhere; but the meat and the liquor were better served there than I have ever seen them in any other place. . . .'"

Only the brain of the man who saw things thus could describe that clear day in May.

June

I

It was a country of deep, calm pastures and slow streams that might have been in England, except that smiling women at the last farm I had passed were talking in Welsh and calling one another Mary Margaret, or Blodwen, or Olwen; and that far off, like a dim thought or a half-forgotten dream, a mountain conversed with the most distant clouds.

Along my path there had been many oaks and doves among their leaves; and deep hedges that sent bragging stems of briers far out over the foot-path, and hid delicate single coils of black bryony in their shadows; and little bridges of ferny stone, and beneath them quiet streams that held flower and tree and cloud in their depth, as if in memory; and great fields where there was nothing, or perhaps a merry, childlike, scampering stoat that pursued a staring, trotting rabbit. I had walked for ten miles and had not seen a man. But it would be more just to ignore such measurements, since the number of milestones was unimportant; so also were the hours. For the country had given me the freedom of time. Dreams of brains that had long been dead became stronger than the strong right hand of to-day and of yesterday. And without asking, these verses sang themselves in my head :—

> Midways of a walled garden,
>   In the happy poplar land,
>   Did an ancient castle stand,
> With an old knight for a warden. . . .
>
> Across the moat the fresh west wind
>   In very little ripples went;
>   The way the heavy aspens bent
> Towards it, was a thing to mind.
>
> The painted drawbridge over it
>   Went up and down with gilded chains;
>   'Twas pleasant in the summer rains
> Within the bridge-house there to sit.

There were five swans that ne'er did eat
   The water weeds, for ladies came
   Each day, and young knights did the same,
And gave them cakes and bread for meat.

I remembered them with a curious sense of
being uncontrolled, or, if you will, of being con-
trolled as one is in sleep, and not by friends, rail-
ways, clothes, and meals, as one usually is. I had
entered that golden age that is always with us,
where there are no wars except in the *Iliad* and
Paradise Lost. At one stile, I saw Aeneas,—in
mediæval mail,—revealing a blue-eyed, confident
face, with a slippery mouth set firm by his destiny.

The country was without obvious character.
An artist could have made nothing of it. Nothing
in the arrangement of meadow and corn-land, wood
and reedy water, made a clear impression on the
mind : they might, perhaps, have been rearranged
without attracting attention. So the landscape
occupied the eyes little and the mind not at all.
Wandering over it with no emotion but rest, I
made of it what I would. In different moods I
might have met there Proserpina, or Camilla, or
Imogen. But chiefly I met there the vague
persons of poetry, like Shelley's Ione, which are
but as large eyes or eloquent lips discerned in

fleeting darkness. And I was too deeply lost to
be at once rescued by the sight of a dignified,
untenanted house, whose shrubberies I wandered
into, along a rabbit run as deep as a footpath
in the short, hawkweedy grass. Docks and
milk - thistles had not yet overpowered lupin
and phlox in the deep borders that still had a
tinge of race in their order and luxuriance. The
martins of the eaves had added to the pompous
portico of the house, so that it had the look of
wild rock. The roses had sent up enormous
talons from their roots and tyrannised everywhere.
There were no flowers in the garden more delicate
than the enchanter's nightshade and nipplewort of
the shrubbery, and the short wild poppies that
could just flower in the old gravel of the paths.
For this one moment the wild and the cultivated
were at peace together, and the harmony gave the
place an unreality,—so that even at the time I had
a dim belief that I was in a garden out of a book,—
which made it a fit haven for my mood. Then, in
a corner, among ruined, ivy-covered elms, I found
a stupid, mournful grotto of wildly-shaped stones
wildly accumulated : at the threshold lay a penny
doll that played a part between comedy and tragedy
very well. Going near, I saw, not quite so clearly

as I see it now, a long-bearded, miserable man, reclining, with fair, unwrinkled brow and closed eyes and shining teeth. On his long sloping forehead a high-mounted spider dreamed; yet he did not stir. A snake, in a fold of his coat beneath his beard, disregarded the heaving of his chest. His breath filled the grotto as a cow's would have done, and it was sweet. And I turned away suddenly, put to shame by what my soul, rather than my eyes, had recognised as Pan. For I ought to have been prepared and I was not.

And as I walked home in an embowered lane, some floating, clashing insects troubled me, and that night, whilst I enjoyed the coming on of sleep, I could not but fancy that I heard the whisper of a god's garment, and wondered had I troubled a god's meditation and walk.

II

To-day, it is another country, as different from the last as old age from maturity. No longer does the greenfinch in the hawthorn say a hundred times that it has five young ones and is happy. No longer does the perfect grass, seen betwixt the boles of beeches, burn against the sky. For that dream of mountains has come true, and so many and so great are they that I can compare my loneliness only with what I have fancied to be the loneliness of one planet that now is and again is not in a tumultuous, grey, midnight sky, or of a light upon a ship between clouds and angry sea, far off.

The thought of steam and electricity never truly touches the primitive sense of distance; and here, even the milestones among the foxgloves are somewhat insolent, when they say that the town under that farthest hill is thirty miles away; for the hill, unknown to me, is farther away than any place I have ever seen, and I would rather say that it is thirty years away and in the dim future or the dim past.

In their shape, there is something human, or suggesting human work, in these hills. Castles, or less noble masonry, noble when fallen, look thus in their ruins, and become thus tricked with delicate verdure and flowers. A great plough driven at random through frosty country would have turned up half-mile clods like these. And at twilight there is a ridge like an extended giant with raised knees and chin thrown back; and often I have seen a horned summit, like a Pan, capture the white moon.

This mountain ahead is not only old, but with its uncovered rock and broken boulders and hoary streams and twisted trees, that look as if a child had gathered garlands and put them in play upon the ancient stems, it declares mightily, if vaguely, the immense past which it has seen. There are English hills which remind us that this land also was once in Arcady : they are of a golden age,— the age of Goldsmith, of Walton, of Chaucer if you like, or of Theocritus ; but they speak of nothing since ; they bear no wrinkles, no wounds, no trophies. But by this mountain you cannot be really at ease until in some way you have travelled through all history. For it has not been as nothing to it that Persia, Carthage, Greece and Rome, and Spain have been great and are not. It has been worn by the footprints of time which have elsewhere but made the grass a little deeper or renewed the woods. It has sat motionless, looking on the world ; it has grown wrinkled ; it is all memory. Were it and its fellows to depart, we should not know how old we were ; for we should have only books. Therefore I love it. It offers no illusions. Its roads are winding and rough. The grass is thin ; the shelter scarce ; the valley crops moderate ; the cheese and mutton good ;

the water pure; the people strong, kind, intelligent,
and without newspapers; the fires warm and bright
and large, and throwing light and shadow upon
pewter and brass and oak and books. It offers
no illusions; for it is clear, as it is not in a city or
in an exuberant English county, that the world
is old and troubled, and that light and warmth and
fellowship are good. Sometimes comes a thought
that it is a huge gravestone, so is it worn, so
obscure and brief its legend. It belongs to the
past, to the dead; and the dead, as they are more
numerous, so here they are greater than we, and
we only great because we shall one day be of their
number. You cannot look at it without thinking
that the time will come when it may be, and we
are not, nor the races of men—

> sed haec prius fuere : nunc recondita
> senet quiete.

And hearing an owl among its oak trees, its age
was quaintly expounded to me by that passage in
the *Mabinogion* where the Eagle of Gwernabwy
seeks a wife.

"The Eagle of Gwernabwy had been long
married to his wife, and had by her many children.
She died, and he continued a long time a widower;
but at length he proposed a marriage with the Owl

of Cwm Cawlwyd. But afraid of her being young, so as to have children by her, and thereby degrade his own family, he first of all went to inquire about her age amongst the aged of the world. Accordingly he applied to the Stag of Rhedynfre, whom he found lying close to the trunk of an old oak, and requested to know the Owl's age.

" ' I have seen,' said the Stag, ' this oak an acorn, which is now fallen to the ground through age, without either bark or leaves, and never suffered any hurt or strain, except from my rubbing myself against it once a day, after getting up on my legs ; but I never remember to have seen the Owl you mention younger or older than she seems to be at this day. But there is one older than I am, and that is the Salmon of Glynllifon.'

" The Eagle then applied to the Salmon for the age of the Owl. The Salmon answered, ' I am as many years old as there are scales upon my skin, and particles of spawn within my belly ; yet never saw I the Owl you mention but the same in appearance. But there is one older than I am, and that is the Blackbird of Cilgwri.'

" The Eagle next repaired to the Blackbird of Cilgwri, whom he found perched upon a small stone, and inquired of him the Owl's age.

"'Dost thou see this stone upon which I sit,' said the Blackbird, 'which is now no bigger than what a man can carry in his hand? I have seen this very stone of such weight as to be a sufficient load for a hundred oxen to draw, which has suffered neither rubbing nor wearing, save that I rub my bill on it once every evening, and touch the tips of my wings on it every morning, when I expand them to fly; yet I have not seen the Owl either older or younger than she appears to be at this day. But there is one older than I am, and that is the Frog of Mochno Bog; and if he does not know her age, there is not a creature living that does know it.'

"The Eagle went last of all to the Frog, and desired to know the Owl's age. He answered, 'I never ate anything but the dust from the spot which I inhabit, and that very sparingly; and dost thou see these great hills that surround and overawe this bog where I lie? They are formed only of the excrements from my body since I have inhabited this place; yet I never remember to have seen the Owl but an old hag, making that hideous noise Too-hoo-hoo, always frightening the children of the neighbourhood.'"

Farther along the road, and not wholly cut off

from a world of richer fields, there is the ruin of
an abbey, which, being the work of human hands,
says the same thing more clearly. It is but a cave
of masonry topped by umbrageous ivy that swells
over its edge like froth over a tankard. Altar
and bells and books and large abbatic oven are
gone. Only the jackdaw remains. The winds
blow through and through the ruins. There is
moss; here are flowers,—yellow cistus and cinque-
foil, purple fumitory, pearly eyebright, and still
some white stitchwort stars. But nothing dies
save what we let die, and here, as in a library, on
this once consecrated ground, meet all religions.
It has room for the Druid. Its ivy leaves repeat
the praises of moon and sun. It will deny no
fairy and no god an altar and a place for dancing.
I have gone there with many fancies and many
memories of books, and there they find a home.
And if, as some have done, you go there with
willingness and an inability to accept what dreams
have hitherto been dreamed, you may seem there,—
in favourable hours, when the casements of all the
senses are opening wide upon eternity, and all
things are silent as fishes, and the curves of bramble
and brier among the masonry seem to be thinking,
—to be on the edge of a new mythology and to

taste the joy of the surmises of him who first saw
Pan among the sedges or the olives.

July

I

For three days I walked and drove towards
Llyn-y-Fan Fach. On the first day I passed through
a country of furnaces and mines, and the country
had been exquisitely made. The gently swirling
lines of hill and valley spoke of the mountains far
off, as the little waves and the foam coming up
the shore like chain-mail speak of the breakers out
in the bay. Every large field that was left un-
burdened by house or factory had a fair curve in it,
and even the odd pieces of land were something
more than building sites and suggested their con-
text. But as we passed through, only the highest
points gave the curious eye any satisfaction, since
the straight lines of houses, the pits and the heaps
of refuse, and the enormous factories, obscured
the true form of the land. Even so might some
survivor of a deluge look upon the fair land he
knew ; for we lacked the courage to think of hill
and valley as having undergone an inevitable
change, which in a century might be known to

have brought beauty with it, as changes do. Everything was brand-new, but not fresh. A wanton child might have done it all, had he been large and rich and careless enough to do it thus, *nec numero nec honore*. Or had it been all built to the music of the organ-grinder whom I met playing, for the joy of playing, "The Absent-minded Beggar"? The staring, mottled houses of various stone and brick, which had no character save what comes of perfect lack of character, might have been made by some neglected boy who had only played with penny trains and motor cars and steamers and bicycles. Phlox and foxglove, and sweet-william and snapdragon, and campanula and amber lilies could not make sweet the "rockeries" of hot-looking waste. The streets, named after factory magnates, had been made in long blocks and broken up by the boy, thoughtlessly. The factories themselves, noble as some of the furnaces were by day and night when sweating men moved to and fro before them, were of the same origin. They were mere cavities, and one marvelled that the smoke from their chimneys was permitted to waver and roll in the same way as clouds the most splendid and august. Many were already in places decayed. That they had been glazed only to have the

windows pierced by the stones of happy children
was all in their favour that could be seen. Their
roofs had fallen in, and neither moss nor ivy had
had time to grow thereon; the splintered wood
was still new and white. Middle-aged men of
fifteen and aged men of thirty were in keeping
with their ludicrous senility. A millionaire playing at imitating antiquity could have done no
worse. The decay was made in Birmingham.
Time had been sweated and had done its work
very ill. Here and there, indeed, there were
scenes which perhaps an unprejudiced mind would
have found sublime. There were pools, for example, filled with delicate grass and goldfish
amongst it. They were made yesterday, and yet
had they fed little brooks for ages they could not
have been more shining and serene as sunset poured
all its treasury into their depths. Passing one,
soon after dawn, and before the night-workers had
left the factory, the reeds in it stood up just so that
no storied pool had more the trick of antiquity.
Near by, one green field, set amidst houses and a
factory, was enclosed by abundant but ill-stretched
barbed wire, without gate or possible entrance of any
kind. In the middle was a tattered notice, warning
trespassers. No cloister was ever more inviolate.

The grass grew as it liked, and all whom the heavy headstones of the buildings had spared in the rash burial of rural divinities must there have danced; and the grass shone as if with recent festival, and its emptiness hinted at a recent desertion. All the other fields had been carelessly defaced by broken cheap china and tin kettles and rags, and like cattle that have a day to live and are insulted with the smell of their lucky companions' blood, they were dreary and anxious. Footmarks, but not one footpath, crossed them in all directions. . . . A Battersea kitchen after Christmas is adorned like this land with similar spoiled toys. Their pathos is the same in kind; but here it is worse, because a grown-up person—the original grandeur and antiquity of the land as shown in the one green field—has burst in and marred the completeness of the children's play.

II

At the edge of one village in this country there was a new public-house, the worst of the buildings in the place, because the most impudent. It glittered and stank and was called "The Prince of Wales." Inside, English and some Welsh voices were singing together all of Britain's most loved songs; perhaps "Dolly Gray" predominated, and

in its far-floating melody the world-sorrow found
a voice; for a harper played on the harp while
they sang. The landlord liked to have the harper
there, because he drew customers and kept them,
and it was clear that he himself, when he had time,
loved music, since he took his pipe out of his
mouth to hum the last words of a song about a
skylark, a dead mother, and some angels. The
next song was "The Rising of the Lark," which
begins thus :

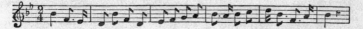

No one sang except the harper; the landlord
frowned, remarked that "Evan was very drunk to-
night," and offered to stop the song if we objected,
and then began to talk. He said that the harper
was a poor sort of man; had been a schoolmaster
and was a "scholar"; had been to prison for an
unmentioned crime; and was now a man with a
wife, whom he supported by odd jobs and by "my
own charity, for," explained the host, "I let him
have his drinks free." He was fond of his harp,
as if it had been a horse or a barrel of beer; and
boasted, when drunk, that he knew that he was
the sixth of his family who had played the harp,
and that same harp, and that he was the last of the

true harpers. So we went into the taproom and sat down with fourteen miners and the harper, who was doing his best with "God bless the Prince of Wales."

"You are fond of your National Anthem," said a voice which might have cut glass and perhaps came from Glasgow.

Whereupon, with sublime, gentle anger the harper played and sang the National Anthem of Wales :—

Mae hen wlad fy Nhadau yn anwyl i mí, Gwlad beirdd a chantorion, en-wogion o fri; Ei gwrol ry - fel - wyr, gwlad - garw - yr tra mad, Dros ryddid goll - a - sant eu gwaed. Gwlad! Gwlad! pleid - iol wyf i'm Gwlad, Tra môr yn fur i'r bur hoff bau, O bydded i'r hen-iaith ba - rhau.

The words cannot, of course, be translated, but the following are as much like them as a photograph of Snowdon is like Snowdon. "Dear to me is the old land of my fathers, a land of bards and minstrels of great name. Her brave warriors, best of patriots, poured out their blood for freedom. Ancient and mountainous Wales, Paradise of the bard, every valley and cliff is lovely in my sight; through the feeling of patriotism, how alluring is the ripple on her rivers and brooks. If the enemy treads my country under foot, the old language of the Welsh lives as it used to live; the Muse suffers not, in spite of the horrid hand of the traitor, nor yet the melodious harp of my country." And the chorus says: "My country, my country, I am bound up with my country. While the sea is a boundary to the fair and well-loved place, may the old language last." . . .

While he sang, we saw that the harper was a little, pale, snub-nosed, asthmatic man, with red hair and a delicate, curved mouth and heavy-lidded, pathetic, sentimental, but unsympathetic grey eyes, and glowing white fingers. He leaned over his instrument as a mother over her child when she is bathing it, or as a tired man reaping with a reaping-hook. He evidently knew what he liked; yet, as the evening wore out, he lost himself sentimentally over the poorest tunes. He seemed to love listening at least as well as playing. Slowly we emptied the house of all its Englishmen by encouraging him to play the airs which the harp had known

through all its life. He played the plaintive best.
Such quick happiness as " New Year's Eve," which
begins—

moved his sorrow more and his sentiment less, and
his white fingers stuck among the strings.

When he rose at 11 P.M. to go, he could carry
the harp, but hardly himself ; and we led him home,
murmuring sad ditties lovingly. As he stumbled
in, he cursed his wife, a frail burden of middle age,
singularly like himself, and then continued to
murmur.

The light of one candle and the beauty of the
harp almost made beautiful the room in which we
stood, while he sat with his instrument.   The
garish wall-paper was mildewed with lovely gleaming white fur, near the windows ; elsewhere it was
decorated by a large tradesman's photograph of Mr.
Chamberlain, a copy of "The Maiden's Prayer,"
and the usual framed mourning verses on relatives ; there was, too, a plush mandoline, and in the
hearth a frond of the royal fern, and over it photographs of two generations of big consumptive men.

For a time the harper hesitated between the
English tunes which were most in favour at " The

Prince of Wales" and the songs for which the harp
was made, when it was made for a bard who could
string a harp, make a song for it, and accompany
himself on the strings.   We praised the Welsh airs,
and though he seemed to ignore us, he played
nothing else. We saw only his eyes, his white flickering fingers, and the harp, and as the triumphant,
despairing, adoring melodies swept over it, this
foolish casket of a man seemed to gather up all
that could live of the lovers and warriors of a thousand years. No epitaph could be so eloquent of
transient mortality. He had but to cloud or
brighten those cruel, sentimental eyes, and to
whisper to the dead instrument, to utter all that
they had ever uttered. To this heir had come the
riches of many hearts and he squandered them in a
taproom for beer, and here for our amusement, as if
they had been no better than gold and he a spend-
thrift. When sometimes he paused and silence
came, or only the bark of a pump was heard, we
seemed to have been assisting at the death and the
last carouse of the souls for whom the music spoke.
They lived only in his fingers and the harp, and with
these they must die. They were as fleeting as pale
butterflies in storm or as the Indian moonflower
that blossoms only after sunset in May. Yet again

and again the fingers and the harp consented to
their life, and reassured, and half-believing that,
because he had so much in trust, he could not die,
we sat down and fell asleep, and waking again, were
not surprised to find, as the July dawn approached,
that the harper was harping still.   For in that holy
light that twittered among the strings, he was an
immortal harper, doomed for ever to go on, because
there was so much to be done, and because, as the
landlord had said, he was the last of his race.

III

I went on, and was over the edge of this
country, "built to music and so not built at all,"
when the sun began to rise behind me.   Before, a
range of hills stood up against the cold sky with
bold lines such as a happy child will draw who has
much paper and a stout crayon, and looked so that
I remembered the proverb which says, that if a man
goes up Cader Idris at night, by dawn he is dead,
or mad, or a poet.   They were immense ; they filled
half the sky ; yet in the soft light that felt its way
glimmeringly, and as if fearfully, among their vast
valleys and along their high crags, they looked like
ruins of something far more mighty ; the fields also,
on this side of them, and all the alder-loving streams

and massy woods, were but as the embers of something which the night had made and had only half
destroyed before its flight.   And it was with surprise
that, as I took my eyes off the prospect and looked
down and in the hedge, I saw that I was in a place
where lotus and agrimony and vetch were yellow,
and the wild rose continued as ever to hesitate
between red and white.

It was not long possible to turn my back upon
the rising sun, and when I looked round, I saw
that the country I had left had been taken into the
service of the dawn and was beautiful two miles
away.   Factory and chimney and street were bent
in a rude circle round the sun, and were as the
audience of some story-teller, telling a new tale—
silent, solemn, and motionless, round a fire; and
over them the blue clouds also were silent, solemn,
and motionless, listening to the same tale, round
the sun.

When I went on towards the hills, they by
that time looked as if they had never known the
night; and sweet it was to pass, now and then, a
thatched, embowered cottage, with windows open
to the scented air, and to envy the sleepers within,
while I could see and recognise the things—the sky
and earth and air, the skylarks singing among the

fading stars, and the last cuckoo calling in the silent, vast and lonely summer land—which make dreamless sleep amidst them so divine, I had long not known why. For half the day there was nothing to remember but sudden long views that led, happily, nowhere, among the clouds or the hills, and farms with sweetly smiling women, and jutting out of every hedge-bank a little *pistyll* of fair water, curving and shining in the heat, over a slice of stone or through a pipe, into the road. These things the memory has to work to remember. For, in truth, the day was but as a melody heard and liked. A child who, in the Welsh story, went to the land of the fairies, could only say that he had been listening to sweet airs, when he returned after a long stay.

But at length, when I was among the hills, the ferns whispered all along the stony hedges, and on a cold stream of wind came the scent of invisible hay, and a great drop of rain shook all the bells on a foxglove stalk, and the straight, busy rain came down, and the hills talked with the heavens while it thundered heavily. The doves and jays only left the hedge as I passed within reach of them. The crouching partridge did not stir even after her eye caught mine. The lightning was as a tree of fire growing on the northern sky. The valley below

was a deep and tranquil mere, in which I saw a
church and trees and fields, as if they were reflections of things in the sky, and, like reflections in
water, they were reverend in their beauty. The
rain in my face washed off more than the weariness
of a long day's walk, and I rejoiced, and found it
easy to catch a train six miles off, which had seemed
impossible.

IV

On the next day I was near the lake, Llyn-
y-Fan Fach, and high up among hills, which had in
many places outgrown their grassy garments, and
showed bare cliffs, senates of great boulders, and
streams of sliding fragments of stone like burnt
paper. The delicate mountain sheep were panting
in the heat, or following the shifting oasis of a
shadow that sometimes moved across the hill; a
horse stood nervously still, envying the shadow
which he cast upon the ground. The world, for
hours, was a hot, long road, with myself at one
end and the lake at the other, when gradually I
descended into a gentle land again.

Far off, church bells were celebrating the peace
and beauty of the morning as I turned into a lane
of which more than twenty yards were seldom
visible at one time; and I lost sight of everything

else. Tall hedgerow elms and orchard trees held blue fragments of the sky among their leaves and hid the rest. Here and there was a cottage among the trees, and it seemed less the work of human hands than the cordon and espalier trees, apple and pear, and the fan-shaped cherry on the wall, with glowing bark. July, which had made the purple plum and the crimson bryony berry, had made it also, I thought. The lane was perhaps long enough to occupy an hour of the most slow-paced tranquil human life. Even if you talked with every ancient man that leaned on his spade, and listened to every young linnet that was learning to sing in the hazels, you could not spend more than two hours in passing along it. Yet, more than once, as I was pausing to count the white clusters of nuts or to remind myself that here was the first pale-blue flower of succory, I knew that I took up eternity with both hands, and though I laid it down again, the lane was a most potent, magic thing, when I could thus make time as nothing while I meandered over many centuries, consulting many memories that are as amulets. And even as I walked, the whole of time was but a quiet, sculptured corridor, without a voice, except when the tall grasses bowed and powdered the nettles with seed at my

feet. For the time I could not admit the existence
of strident or unhappy or unfortunate things. I
exulted in the knowledge of how cheaply purchased
are these pleasures, exulted and was yet humiliated
to think how rare and lonely they are, nevertheless.
The wave on which one is lifted clear of the foam
and sound of things will never build itself again.
And yet, at the lane's end, as I looked back at the
long clear bramble curves, I will confess that there
was a joy (though it put forth its hands to an
unseen grief) in knowing that down that very lane
I could never go again, and was thankful that it
did not come rashly and suddenly upon the white
highroad, and that there is no such thing known
to the spirit as a beginning and an end. For not
without cool shadow and fragrance was the white
highroad.

Then, after some miles up a hot and silent hill, I
came to the lake under the chin of a high summit,
and it was cool. . . .

At the end of the twelfth century, when Owen
Gwynedd in the north and Lord Rhys in the
south made little of English kings, a farmer's
widow lived with one son at Blaensawdde, near
the lake. She sent her cattle on to the Black
Mountain under the care of her son. And the

cattle liked Llyn-y-Fan because the great stones on its shore gave them shade, and because the golden stony shallows were safe and sweet, and no water was finer than that in the little quiet wells of the Sawdde brook.

Watching his cattle there one day, the youth saw a lovely girl, with long, yellow hair and pale, melancholy face, seated on the surface of the lake and looking down into the mirror of the water, for she was combing her hair. Some say that she was rowing with golden sculls up and down the lake in a golden boat, so ample was her hair. The young man was moved by her loveliness to hold out to her his own barley-bread and cheese, which was all that he had with him. And she came near, but she would not accept the food; when he tried to touch her, she slid away, saying—

> " O thou of the crimped bread,
> 'Tis not easy to catch me " ;

and so disappeared, as a lily when the waves are rising.

The youth told his adventure to his mother, who advised him to take unbaked dough for the girl, instead of his crisp barley bread.

The next morning he was at the lake before dawn, and saw cold ripples on the water and a

cloud on the highest of the hills.   But as the light
overcame the cloud and began to warm the ripples,
he saw some of his cattle in danger on the steep
side of the lake, where the rains run almost per-
pendicularly down to the margin and cut weals of
naked red earth in the mountain-side.   And as he
was running round to the cattle, he saw the girl
upon the water, and again held out his hand to offer
his unbaked dough.   Again she refused, and said :

> " O thou of the moist bread,
> I will not have thee."

Then, with smiles, she disappeared.

The youth told his second adventure to his
mother, and she advised him to take slightly baked
bread.   The Welsh have a proverb : " Better is
cookery than kingship "; and she being skilled
with the oven, baked him the bread.

The next morning he was again at the lake.
The cold ripples turned to gold and then to silver,
and the cloud left the mountain ; and he saw the
wind making grey O's and V's on the water, until
it was almost evening, and behind him the oak
trees in the Sawdde valley gleamed where his
homeward way would be, when he saw several
cows walking on the water, and then the girl
moving towards him.   He ran forward into the

water; he held out the bread, and she took it, and promised to marry him on the condition that he should not give her three causeless blows; if he did, she would disappear. Suddenly she left him, and he would have cast himself in with despair, if she had not returned with another as beautiful and in the same way, together with a majestic, tall, and hoary man, who promised to bestow the girl upon him if he could distinguish her.

So the two girls stood before him; and the youth, casting down his eyes in thought and perplexity, saw one thrust her little foot forward, and he noticed how her sandals were tied, because he had before studied the beauty of her ankles and feet; and he chose rightly. The old man promised that they should have as many cattle, horses, sheep, and goats as she could count of each without drawing breath. The girl counted quickly, 1, 2, 3, 4, 5, 1, 2, 3, 4, 5, and so on, and all the beasts came up from the lake; and the young man went with the girl and married her, and lived at Esgair Llaethdy beyond Blaensawdde, and there she bore him three sons.

But one day, when they were to go together to a christening, she was reluctant, saying that it was too far to walk; and he bade her take a horse. She asked for her gloves, and when he returned with them, he found her still delaying, and flicked her shoulder with one and said pettingly, "Go, go." And she reminded him that he had given her a causeless blow.

On another day, at a wedding, she gave way to tears, and he tapped her shoulder to admonish her. And she reminded him that he had given her two causeless blows.

Many years later, at a funeral, she laughed, and again he tapped her shoulder. And she turned, and called her cattle and horses and sheep and goats by name—the brindled cow, the white speckled, the mottled, the white-faced cows;

> "And the grey Geingen
> With the white bull
> From the court of the king;
> And the little black calf
> Though suspended on the hook,
> Come thou also quite well home";

and the four grey oxen ploughing in the fields. They followed her to the lake, and behind them grew the furrow made by the plough which the four oxen still drew, and they all entered the lake.

Her sons desired to see her, and she appeared again to her son Rhiwallon, and told him that he was to be a healer of men, and gave him prescriptions, and promised that if he needed her, she would come again. So she often met them near the lake, and once walked with them towards Myddfai, as far as Pant-y-Meddygon, where she showed them herbs and their virtues. And they became famous, and good physicians. They were physicians to Rhys Gryg of South Wales; and the last of their descendants who practised at Myddfai was buried in 1739 at Myddfai church.

August

I

On a fine, very hot day I had to wait three hours for a train, and should have left the bald junction for that time, if I had not seen there a poet of my acquaintance, contentedly reading Spenser on the central platform. I sat down with him, but he preferred reading to talking, and I looked over his shoulder to read:

> Begin then, O my dearest sacred Dame!
> Daughter of Phœbus and of Memorye . . .

And I could not sufficiently admire his fortitude, until, on the arrival of a train, he left the book on the seat, and walked down alongside the train. It stopped ten minutes, and he talked with persons in three different carriages before it left.   He came back unperturbed, and told me briefly that —— from Patagonia was in the train, with —— the bard from North Wales, and a friend from London.   Seeing me surprised, he explained that every Saturday in the summer he spent entirely on the platform, waiting for surprises of this kind.   Four trains stopped there before I left, and each seemed to be laden with friends and acquaintances,—some who lived in distant parts and even overseas, and some whom he had not seen for years.   And some of the persons whom he greeted he had never seen before, which was a good reason for greeting them; he had perhaps heard of them, or they of him; and so they talked.

The liking of Welshmen for Welshmen is very strong, and that not only when they meet on foreign soil, as in London, but in their own land. They do not, I suppose, love their neighbours more than other men do, but when they meet a fellow-countryman for the first time they seem to have a kind of surprise and joy, in spite of the commonness of such meetings.   They do not acquiesce in the fact that the man they shake hands with is of their race, as English people do.   They converse

readily in trains : they are all of one family, and
indeed if you are Welsh, not only can you not avoid
meeting relatives, but you do not wish to. Small
news about the coming and going of people travels
among them rapidly, and I have never got out of
a train in Wales without feeling that I shall meet
some one whom I should like to meet, on the
platform or in the first street. They like their own
land in the same way. I do not easily believe in
patriotism, in times of peace or war, except as a
party cry, or the result of intoxication or an article
in a newspaper, unless I am in Wales.

I did not know before that any save sellers of
newspapers were happy in railway stations, and as
my train went out, I passed the poet at his Spenser
again and recalled the poem called " Howell's
Delight," which was written by a young, unfortunate prince of North Wales in the twelfth
century :—

> A white foam-crowned wave flows o'er the grave
> Of Rhuvawn Bevyr, chief of Rulers.
> I this day hate England, a flat and inactive land,
> With a people involved in every wile ;
> I love the land where I had the much-desired gift of mead,
> Where the shores extend in tedious conflict ;
> I love the society and the numerous inhabitants
> Therein, who, obedient to their Lord,
> Direct their views of peace ;

I love its sea-coast and its mountains,
Its cities bordering on its forests, its fair landscapes,
Its dales, its waters, and its vales,
Its white seamews, and its beauteous women;
I love its warriors, and its well-trained steeds,
Its woods, its strongholds, and its social domicile;
I love its fields clothed with tender trefoil,
Where I had the glory of a lasting triumph;
I love its cultivated regions, the prerogative of heroism,
Its far extended wilds, and its sports of the chase,
Which, Son of God! are great and wonderful.
How sleek the majestic deer, and in what plenty found;
I achieved with a push of a spear the task of honour
Between the Chief of Powys and fair Gwynedd;
And if I am pale in the rush of conflict,
'Tis that I know I shall be compelled to leave my country,
For it is certain that I cannot hold out till my party comes,
A dream has revealed it, and God says 'tis true.
A white foam-crowned wave flows o'er the grave,
A white bright-foaming wave boldly raves against the towns,
Tinted the time it swells like glittering hoar.
I love the marches of Merioneth,
Where my head was pillowed on a snow-white arm;
I love the nightingale on the privet wood
In the famous vale of Cymmer Deuddwfr,
Lord of heaven and earth, the glory of Gwyneddians.
Though it is so far from Keri to Caerliwelydd,
I mounted the yellow steed, and from Maelienydd
Reached the land of Reged between night and day.
Before I am in the grave, may I enjoy a new blessing
From the land of Tegyngyl of fairest aspect!

II

The flowers by the road, wood-betony, sage,
mallow, ragwort . . . were dry; the larches, that

were fitted to the hillside like scales or breast feathers, were dry; but a mountain stream, which many stones tore to ribbons, was with me for miles, and to the left and to the right many paths over the hills ran with alluring courses for half a mile, like happy thoughts or lively fancies, and ended suddenly. The mountains increased in height as the sun sank, and their sides began to give a home to enormous, still shadows and to rich, inaccessible groves among the clefts. And in the end of the afternoon I came to a village I knew, which grew round an irregular lawn.

From the inn, I could see the whole village.

The limes before me were full of light; the green grass beyond was tending to be grey. There were not far fewer people than usual in the neighbourhood, yet the calm was great. It seemed to have something to announce and to call solemnly for silence; the voice of a child crying, a man with shining cuffs, was an extraordinary impertinence.

But two reclining cows were calm enough, and in the middle distance an oak was stately enough. A tramp, his wife, and five children spoke with quiet, husky voices that were sad enough. A passage from *Hyperion* which I recalled was noble enough. Six bells that rang three miles off and some white downs of cloud on the horizon were in harmony. It was a time when the whole universe strove to speak a universal speech, the speech of the stars in their courses, of the flower that is beautiful, of the soul that aspires, of the mind that thinks. But, as it seemed, owing to my fault, the effort was unsuccessful, and I rose hurriedly and left the village behind.

III

And while the hedgerows on one side of the road were in places rich with the heavy, horizontal sunshine that came through gateways on the other side, I saw the star-like shining of the windows of an old house on a hill. A difficult winding lane led up to it, and so long was the lane that between the road and the house a badger and a raven had their homes. When I came near the house one pallid angle of it glowed, and only where it glowed was it visible.

The house was perhaps two hundred years old—stately, grey as the old blackthorns in the hedge, and it was, perhaps because I knew of the fading race that had lived within it, the oldest thing among those old hills. It was more unchangeable than the most grim crag on the hills which had its

milkwhite harebell on that day. It was a survival
from winter, from hundreds of winters, and therefore, though young in years, it spoke a language
which time, knowing that the unchangeable is
dead, had forgotten:

> A spirit calling in an old old tongue
> Forgotten in lost graves in lonesome places;
> A spirit huddled in an old old heart
> Like a blind crone crouched o'er a long-dead fire. . . .

Nothing ever happened among the Powells at
——. The lawn was mowed; the fern from the hill
was carted down; the little red apples ripened; the
Powell hair turned from gold to grey. A stranger,
indeed, heard much of them, but when he asked
where they lived, he was told that there were
thirty of them in the church and one at —— on
the hill. Five generations of them had lived there,
since the only conspicuous one of the family had
died in the first war with Napoleon. Of those
five, the last could only say that theirs had been
the most desperate of quests, for they knew not
what they sought. They had lived in dignity and
simplicity, neither sporting nor cultured, yet loving
foxhounds and books. Generation after generation of the children had learned " L'Allegro " and
" Il Penseroso " from their fathers, and with all

their happiness in that dim house, they learned to love " Il Penseroso " best. . . .

September

In the afternoon I climbed out of a valley, descended again, and came on to a road that rolled over many little hills into many little valleys, and at the top of each hill grew the vision of a purple land ahead. But, for some miles, the valleys were solitary. There were brooks in them with cold, fresh voices, and copses of oak, and sometimes the smoke or the white wall of a house. There sang the latest of the willow-wrens, and among the blackthorns a bullfinch, with delicate voices. The air was warm and motionless ; the light on oak and grass was steady and rich ; the sky was low and leaning gently to the earth, and its large white clouds moved not, though they changed their shapes. But these things belonged to the brooks, the copses, the willow-wrens ; or so it seemed, since that warm day, which elsewhere might have seemed so kind with an ancient kindness as if to one returning home after long exile, was not kind, but was indifferent and made an intruder of me. And I should have passed the stony hedges and the little brooks over the road and the desolate mine, in the indifferent little worlds of the valleys, one by one, as if they had been in a museum, or as if I had been taken there to admire them, had it not been that on the crests of the road between valley and valley, I saw the purple beckoning hills far away, and that, at length, towards the last act of the dim, rich, long-drawn out and windless sunset, the road took me into a small valley that was different. Just within reach of the sunset light, on one side of the valley lay a farm, with ricks, outhouses, and two cottages, all thatched. In the corner of the field nearest to the house, the long-horned craggy cattle were beginning to lie down. Those cattle, always vast and fierce, seemed to have sprung from the earth—into which the lines of their recumbent bodies flowed—out of which their horns rose coldly and angrily. The buildings also had sprung from the earth, and only prejudice taught me that they were homes of men. They enmeshed the shadows and lights of sunset in their thatch, and were as some enormous lichen-covered things, half crag, half animal, which the cattle watched, together with five oaks.

There was not a sound, until a child ran to a pump, and sang a verse of some grave hymn lightheartedly, and filled a shining can with dark water, and disappeared.

Then I raised my eyes, so that they crept swiftly, though not without feeling the weariness of the distance, over hill after hill to the one upon which the last, mild, enormous, purple dragon of the sunset was pasturing; yet I saw nothing in earth or sky which did not belong to those things, half crag, half animal, in the small valley, in happiness and peace that consented to the voice of the child.

Then I passed the farm and saw a crimson fire casting innumerable arms about a room; I heard the rattle and click of the pump; and I knew that it was cold, that I had far to go, and that the desolation beyond the farm was illimitable.

For such moods of the world are easily shut against us for some small thing, as the world of the little people was shut against the man in the tale which Gerald of Wales repeats :—

A priest of Gower, named Elidorus, told Gerald that when he was a schoolboy he was often beaten by his master. So one day he ran away and hid himself in a hollow among the alder roots at the edge of a stream. There he was safe, but had no food. And on the third day two wonderfully little men came to him and said that if he would come with them, they would lead him to a happy and pleasant country. He therefore left his hiding-place and went with the little men through a country of wood and field and water that was beautiful, although they saw neither sun nor moon. At last they came to the court of the king, and Elidorus was presented to him; and, after looking at him carefully, the king gave him over to his young son. And the people of that country, though they were wonderfully little, were beautiful in shape and of a fair complexion, and they wore long hair that fell over their shoulders in the manner of women. Their horses and hounds were of a suitable size. The little people ate neither flesh nor fish, but lived on milk, which they concocted with saffron. They never took an oath; they always spoke the truth. Nor had they any kind of public worship, but simply kept and loved good faith. And their language was very much like Greek, as he afterwards said.

The little people often went up into our world, and never returned without speaking harshly of men for their ambition and want of faith and con-stancy. Sometimes Elidorus went up with them. Sometimes he went up alone, but revealed himself to his mother only, telling her of his life and of the little people and their country. When he told her that gold abounded there, she asked him to bring her some golden thing as a gift. So he stole a golden ball from the son of the king and ran to his mother with it. But the little people pursued him, and in his haste he stumbled over the threshold of his mother's door and fell. He lost hold of the ball, and the little people picked it up and went away, laughing at him and taunting him. And when he rose up, he was ashamed and angry because he had stolen the ball. Then he would have gone back to the country of the little people, but, although he searched for a year, he could never discover the true path. In course of time he gave up the search and the hope of returning. He even went back to school and became a priest. But long afterwards, when he was an old man, he could never speak of his strange truancy without tears.

October

I

The rain and the wind had ceased, and in the garden the Painted Lady butterflies were tremulously enjoying the blue Michaelmas daisies, and an old man was gathering seeds of hollyhock, evening primrose, and foxglove, and putting them into white cups on the garden paths. In the hedges the bryony coils were crimson and green among thorn and hazel; the sparrows were thick in the elms, whose branches had snatched straws from passing waggons; one bare ash tree was all in bud with singing linnets. Over all was a blue sky, with throbbing clouds of rooks; and beyond all, over leagues of rocky pastures and grim oaks, the mountains,—and upon one of them a white flower of cloud or snow, above which presently rose many clouds, and in the midst of them a narrow pane of sky full of misty golden light, and behind that a land where Troy is still defended,—where still Camilla, loving war and maidenhood eternally, bounds over the unbending corn,—and where, in the hall of a castle, four-and-twenty damsels are embroidering satin, and the least lovely of them is lovelier than Gwenhwyvar, the wife of Arthur, "when she has appeared loveliest at the Offering, or on the day of the Nativity, or at the feast of Easter."

II

The last village was far behind. The last happy chapel-goer had passed me long ago. A cock

crowed once and said the last word on repose.
The rain fell gently; the stems of the hazels in
the thickets gleamed; and the acorns in the grassy
roads, and under the groups of oaks, showed all
their colours, and especially the rosy hues where
they had but just before been covered by the cup.
One by one I saw the things which make the
autumn hedges so glorious and strange at a little
distance: the yellow ash trees, with some green
leaves; the hoary and yellow willows; the hawthorns, purple and crimson and green; the briers,
with most hips where there were fewest leaves;
the green brambles with red fruit and black; tall,
grey, and leafless thistles with a few small crimson
flowers; the grey-green nettles with purple stems;
the ragwort flowers; and on the long, green, wet
grass the fallen leaves shining under red and
yellow oaks; and through the olive lances of hazel
the fields shining in patines of emerald. Doves
cooed in the oaks, pheasants gleamed below. The
air was full of the sweetness of the taste of black-
berries, and the scent of mushrooms and of
crumbling, wild carrot-seeds, and the colour of
yellow, evening grass. The birches up on the hills
above the road were golden, and like flowers.
Between me and them a smouldering fire once or

twice sent up dancing crimson flames, and the colour and perfume of the fire added themselves to the power of the calm, vast, and windless evening, of which the things I saw were as a few shells and anemones at the edge of a great sea. The valley waited and waited.

Then by the roadside I saw a woman of past middle age sitting silently. Her small head was poised a little haughtily on a blithe neck; her fine, grey, careful hair spared gloomy white forehead and round ears, which shone; her full, closed lips spoke clearly of both the sadness of to-day and the voluptuousness of yesterday. She was beautiful, and not merely because she had once been a beautiful girl. She had become mortal through grief, and though I could not see her crown, yet crowned she was.

Will you always, O sad and tranquil Demeter, sit by the wayside and expect Persephone?

III

It was the last day of the month, and in a gently heaving land, which was broken every three or four miles by a sudden, castled crag, Autumn was perfect, but with just a touch of sublimity added to its beauty by the thought that, on the next day or the next, winter would fall upon her unsuspected, as Pizarro and the Spanish cavalry fell upon that noble Indian, Atahualpa, who had come up to them in peace and meekness and pomp, upon a golden litter, among thousands of his gentle subjects, making music and decorated with gold, and expecting to meet the gods.

The bells of the cattle on broad, yellow lawns were ringing. Squirrels glowed in the road; the heavy rooks let fall the acorns among the leaves continually. The last beams of the sun reached now a circle of high bracken on a far-off hill, and reached it alone and transfigured it with strong, quiet light; and then made one brown hill seem to be consumed in a golden glow, while the next hill was sombre; and again devoted themselves to a group of beeches that shone ruddy, branch and leaf and bole, and divine and majestic and unrelated to the cattle passing underneath.

The sun went down; wild-duck and moorhen cried and scudded on the calm, winding, silver river at my feet; and in a field beyond, that retained so much liquid and lugubrious light as to seem a green water, some laughing boys in white and yellow played football, without regarding the silver and purple, frosty sky, to which, nevertheless, their shrill voices added something, from which their movements took something, that was glorious and pathetic. And near by, dark oxen with rocking gait thrust their horns up into the sky as they approached the bridge.

November

The night had almost come, and the rain had not ceased, among the hills of an unknown country. Behind me, twelve desolate miles of hill and sky away, was a village; and on the way to it, half-a-dozen farms; and before me were three or four houses scattered over two or three miles of winding lanes, with an inn and a church. The parson had just come away from his poultry, and as his wife crossed the road with her apron over her head, I asked where the inn was, and whether it had a room ready in the winter. Two minutes after she had seen me—if she could see me in the dark lane—she had told me that if the inn had no room, I was not to go farther, but to stay at the vicarage. But the inn had a bed to spare, and there was good beer to be had by a great fire in a room shining with brass and pewter, and overhead guns and hams and hanks of wool; and the hostess was jocund, stout, and young, and not only talkative but anxious to be talked to, and she had that maternal kindness—or shall I call it the kindness of a very desirable aunt?—towards strangers, which I have always found in Welsh women, young and old, in the villages and on the moors. So there I stayed and listened to the rain and the fire and the landlady's rich, humming voice uttering and playing strange tricks with English. I was given a change of clothing as if I had asked and paid for it. Then I went to the vicarage, and because I said I loved Welsh hymns and Welsh voices, the vicar and his wife and daughter, without unction or preparation or a piano, sang to me, taking parts, some tremendous hymns and some gay melodies,

> Whence banished is the roughness of our years,

which made the rain outside seem April rain. They sang, and told me about the road I was to follow, until I had to go to my inn.

Next day, after paying what I liked at the inn, and promising the hostess that I would learn Welsh, I walked for twenty miles over stony roads gleaming with rain upon the white thorns and bloom on the sloes, and through woods where nothing brooded solemnly over grey moss and green moss on the untrodden, rotten wood, and up dry, ladder-like beds of brooks that served as paths, over peat and brindled grass, and along golden hazel hedges, where grew the last meadow-sweet with herb-robert and harebell and one wild rose, and above little valleys of lichened ash trees ; and sometimes beneath me, and sometimes high above, the yellow birches waved in the rain, like sunset clouds fettered to the ground and striving and caracoling in their fetters.

Again I came at nightfall to a strange farm-house, and was honoured by being asked into the kitchen ; again I was given dry clothes. The juicy mutton broke up like game. The farmer sang to me from the Welsh hymn-book and from a col-lection of old Welsh songs, in a room which was none the worse for a portrait of Miss Maud Millett, "The Soldier's Farewell," and the presence of a fierce-thoughted, mild-eyed young minister, who was the most majestic man I have seen since I first saw the shop-walkers at Maple's—the kind of man whom one supposes that the animals observe, and so learn to temper their contempt for us. This man had the strange whim to call the devil a gentleman, a poor distinction which I could not understand until he showed me a passage, that should be highly interesting to gentlemen and the residue of mankind, in one of the Iolo MSS. Beginning at the beginning, the MS. declares that Adam's eldest son was ungenteel, "a low vassal"; but Seth and Abel were genteel. The angels also, the tenth grade, who fell from heaven, were ungenteel, "through pride, which is the principal characteristic of weakness." Continuing, the writer says of Noah's sons that one was a lord, the second a gentleman, the third a servile clown. Either the usual order of the sons is changed, or Ham was held to be a gentleman because from him was descended Nimrod, and all destroyers are gentlemen. If this be true, then Japheth was a "servile clown,"—in spite of the fact that he was "the first who made a targe with a lake in it, to signify that he and his brothers possessed the whole world," inventing heraldry,—merely in order that ungentility might have a common fount. And thus we see that descent is efficacious to all except descendants of Japheth (or Ham), and that therefore the genealogies are waste paper, and a popular pursuit which has hitherto been regarded as harmless is proved to be also fraudulent. . . . Then he went back to his books, which he allowed me to see. They were pretty, uncut editions of the profane classics; theology, Welsh history, and *Grimm's Fairy Tales*—all thumbed and pencilled.

Frowning above was a photograph of Spurgeon, and a picture of Whitman from a chance number of an English weekly.

When I left on the next morning early, the farmer was threshing with an oaken flail in his barn; but he stepped out to tell me what he knew of the way through the bogs and over the hills,—for there was no road or path,—and to beg me not to go, and to ask me to pay what I had paid at my former inn, for my lodging.

The next twenty miles were the simplest and most pleasant in the world. For nearly the whole way there was a farm in every two miles. I had to call at each to ask my way. At one, the farmer asked me in and sat me by his peat fire to get dry, and gave me good milk and butter and bread, and a sack for my shoulders, and a sense of perfect peace which was only disturbed when he found that I could not help him in the verses he was writing for a coming wedding. At another, the farmer wrote out a full list of the farms and landmarks on my way, lest I should forget, and gave me bread and butter and milk. At another, I had but to sit and get dry and watch an immeasurably ancient, still, and stately woman, her face bound with black silk which came under her

chin like a stock, and moving only to give a smile
of welcome and goodwill. At another, they added
cheese to the usual meal, and made the peat one
golden cone upon the hearth, and brewed a pale
drink which is called tea. Sometimes the shrill-
voiced women, with no English, their hair flying
in the wind, came out and shrieked and waved
directions. In one of the houses I was privileged
to go from the kitchen, with its dresser and
innumerable jugs and four tea-services, to the
drawing-room. It was a change that is probably
more emphasised in Wales than elsewhere, since
the kitchens are pleasanter, the drawing-rooms
more mysterious, than in England, I think. The
room was cold, setting aside the temperature, and
in spite of crimson in the upholstery and cowslip
yellow in the wall-paper and dreary green on the
floor. There was a stuffed heron ; a large pathetic
photograph of man and wife ; framed verses ; some
antimacassars, and some Bibles. . . . The room
was dedicated to the unknown God. The farmer
did not understand it ; he admired it completely,
and with awe, reverencing it as a priest his god,
knowing that it never did him any good, and yet
not knowing what evil might come if he were
without it.

At last, as I left landmarks behind in the rain, I reached a poor little house where a family of sixteen sat round the peat or went about their work, all preserving that easy dignity when their poverty is under the eyes of a stranger which I have ever found among the Welsh. Of his own accord, the farmer came with me over the worst part of my way—two apparently trackless miles—until I came to a road at last. He spoke no English; and yet I had, and think he had, a wonderful sense of satisfaction in our companionship of an hour, as he led me over undulating, boggy lands intersected by rivers,—which looked a little way off like an unpeopled continent in miniature, with lake and hill and stream,—and along the edges of steep crags that rose sheer from black brooks and grey foam, and above hollows inhabited by perfect, golden birches. It was a land which always comes back to me when the same cold rain, on the top of a London omnibus, beats the face and blurs the hurrying crowd and makes the ears tingle. Once, the rain stopped, and the air was calm, as we passed among decaying oaks, which were as a church full of men when the organ begins, and we no better than any one of them. . . . He accepted money with as little offence as the others had given when they refused it. As a rule,

I would rather drop a sovereign by the road than offer a man sixpence who has nothing of the lackey about him, though imitativeness has compelled me to do otherwise.

As he left me, a mist which he had probably foreseen suddenly cloaked me and hid everything except the road and its green edges, where the gentlest of winds shook the rain on the feathered grasses, but could not make it fall. The road was a river, shallow but swift, and for four miles there was not a house visible, except when the mist divided for a minute and showed, far away, a fair, shining, unshadowed valley, and a white house and motionless sheep, which I saw as a departed spirit might for a moment behold the earth; for the world was gone like last year's clouds. Yet again, the mist rose a little and showed lawns with a lovely dim light over the grass, as if the lawns had a light of their own which also made them seem aloof. And strangely sufficient was the mist, the hard road, and the moist stick in my hand, when my mood changed as when at night bells clash as if they were building the cathedral again with their noise, and we watch its pinnacles thus made among the stars, and joyously they clash so that we believe they will never cease; and suddenly they cease and slowly toll. For the inn glimmered close by, and I heard the rustle of many sheep, and my brain began to prepare itself for meeting men again.

December

Twenty miles from the sea, a little river leaves an underground lake, flows through a cave, and falls radiant from the darkness among steep rocks, and takes a course like a man's thoughts when they have the joy of an unknown impulse and no certain aim. There, the river always talks of Spring. It winds and studies all the country round,—castle and farm and inn and old graves,—with many sharp digressions, which I suppose it could not have done without, any more than I in a similar case. Now it shines and curves gently and looks over its bank at the cattle, and now, changing its voice, it is gloomy and intent among mossy stones, and now it leaps and is all foam over a ladder of crag. Suddenly it enters a steep, wooded valley, and falling over a perpendicular cliff, it is richly embowered, and always remembers Summer, and begins to please the trout where it swirls with shuddering foam or runs swiftly in the middle, and gloomily and slow under the alder roots. But in the wood, where birch and oak and hornbeam stand over it, it gains a look of great and growing age which mountain rivers have, and a shadow besets its cheerfulness, so unlike the happy prime of English waters among cowslip meadows. When it leaves the wood it is a masterly, full-grown stream that can turn a mill-wheel. Then it begins to pause in deep pools under shadowy bridges, where the otter slides for a moment over a slippery ledge and then can hide his path for fifty yards. There the girls stand and dip their vessels, and think for a minute while the vessels fill, and raise them again, spilling some, and show that the black water can shine as when it left the mountain ten miles away.

Leaving a hamlet near one bridge, the river runs through such a lonely land that even on stormy nights it is heard only by the groups and groves of oaks that guard the stony and tussocky pastures. Here and there, on either hand, a brook adds a murmur to its music. A throbbing flock of lapwings for ever wheels and gleams and calls over it. The royal fern basks on its edge. And there Autumn abides.

When it reaches the next village, the river is so yellow and poisonous that only in great floods

dare the salmon come up. There, with two other
rivers, it makes a noble estuary, and at the head
of that estuary and in the village that commands
it, the old and the new seem to be at strife.

On the one hand are the magnificent furnaces;
the black, wet roads; the ugly houses, that have
the one pleasing virtue of not pretending to be
anything else, with their naïvely chosen names,
such as " Bryn Gwyn Bach " and Mazawattee Villa;
the cheap and pretentious chapels; yet all of them
filled with people bearing the old names,—the
women called Olwen, Myfanwy, Angharad,—loving
the old songs, theologies, histories. I heard of
one man there who once heard part of *Robinson
Crusoe* told on a winter night. For a year he
struggled and learned to read, and found no version
in Welsh. Then he went to London, and while
he helped to sell milk, learned to read English, and
came back home with a copy of the desirable
book.

On the other hand, there is the great water,
bent as if it were a white arm of the sea, thrust
into the land to preserve the influence of the sea.
Close to the village stands a wooded barrow and an
ancient camp; and there are long, flat marches
where sea-gulls waver and mew; and a cluster of

oaks so wind-worn that when a west wind comes it seems to come from them as they wave their haggish arms; and a little desolate white church and white-walled graveyard, which on December evenings will shine and seem to be the only things at one with the foamy water and the dim sky, before the storm; and when the storm comes the church is gathered up into its breast and is a part of it, so that he who walks in the churchyard is certain that the gods—the gods that grow old and feeble and die—are there still, and with them all those phantoms following phantoms in a phantom land,—a gleam of spears, a murmur of arrows, a shout of victory, a fair face, a scream of torture, a song, the form of some conqueror and pursuer of English kings,—which make Welsh history, so that to read it is like walking in that place among December leaves that seem never to have lived and been emerald, and looking at the oaks in the mist, which are only hollows in the mist, while an ancient wind is ceaselessly remembering ancient things.

INDEX

THE END